ale Publishers Ltd
eet

rsdale.com

und in Finland

-602-2
1-84024-602-5

As a Do

GEORGE POLES & S

su

As a Dodo

The obituaries you'd really like to see

GEORGE POLES & SIMON LITTLEFIELD

Contents

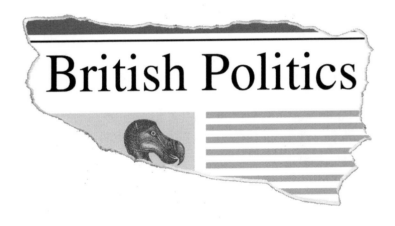

British Politics

100,000 Scottish Votes

3 May 2007–4 May 2007

100,000 Scottish Votes have been cast into the Great Polling Station in the Sky after massed ranks of Scottish ballot papers were spoiled in a debacle on a scale rivalled only by Jeb Bush's 'Hanging Chads 2000' Tour of Florida.

Scottish Votes were born amidst a fanfare of nationalist triumphalism from SNP leader Alex Salmond who predicted a bold new future for Scottish votes, a future in which Scots would determine their own political destiny and no longer migrate to Westminster to bugger things up for the English (a phenomenon believed to be the Scots' revenge for the decades when English votes buggered things up for Scotland with legislation like the poll tax, not to mention all those jokes about deep-fried Mars bars).

Within minutes of the polling stations being opened, however, Scottish voters were thrown into confusion by multiple ballot papers whose complexity was on a par with the Schleswig-Holstein question and whose incomprehensibility was on a par with *Rab C. Nesbitt*. Matters were made yet worse for The Scottish Votes when they found themselves faced by a new method of electronic counting. The new counting machines were to prove disastrous – particularly in the Highlands and Islands where electricity only reaches the communities sporadically, chiefly during lightning strikes.

Meanwhile, in the Western Isles, the count was delayed by fog, which grounded the helicopter carrying the ballot boxes to Stornoway. Ballots had to be transported in the traditional manner, with each vote placed in a bottle and thrown into the sea. Islanders were urged to empty suitable bottles as quickly as possible and cast their votes into one of the two wobbly Atlantic Oceans in front of them.

With initial returns suggesting Boris McYeltsin's election as the Scottish Socialist Party MSP for the constituency of Tommy Sheridan (South) and Nessie being returned as First Minister for Bournemouth, it quickly became apparent that the new system made the calculation of how many votes had been cast and for whom – hitherto understood to be the purpose of elections – even more difficult to add up than the cost of the Scottish Parliament Building.

Less than twenty-four hours after their birth, 100,000 Scottish Votes were found dead, bludgeoned by electoral incompetence. Following a lengthy court process they will be folded (incorrectly) and marked 'spoiled' before being buried at a place of worship, in a service which has not yet been determined, thanks to a funeral ballot form modelled on a National Lottery scratch card.

Boris Johnson's Mouth

1964–2006

Tory frontbencher Boris Johnson's Mouth has passed away during the night, mere hours after being shot off by Mr Johnson himself.

Boris Johnson's Mouth was born in 1964, to a long line of Mouths. Educated at Eton and Oxford, and well-versed in the languages of Ancient Greece, Rome and Billy Bunter, The Mouth had all the qualifications necessary to make it a senior body part at both the influential right-leaning *Daily Telegraph* newspaper and the influential right-leaning *Spectator* magazine. Its progress was swift, soon becoming the *Telegraph* leader writer, a task made all the more difficult by having to grasp its pen between its teeth. Just one year after Mr Johnson's marriage to Marina Wheeler in 1993, it became Mouth to *The Spectator* editor, in which role it divided its time between conducting editorial meetings and whispering sweet nothings into Petronella Wyatt's ear.

Beyond journalism, Boris Johnson's Mouth began to make a name for itself in comedy, appearing on satirical panel shows such as *The News Quiz* and *Have I Got News For You*, as well as in the long running Whitehall farce *The Conservative Party*, in which it was to take a leading role in 2004 as Parliamentary Mouth to the Shadow Minister for Arts. Regretfully, The Mouth was already becoming increasingly eccentric and unreliable and, in October 2004, Mr Johnson is believed to have shot it off for the first time, making characteristically ill-judged reference to the Hillsborough disaster and claiming that Liverpudlians were mawkish. Despite doing dreadful penance by making a speaking tour of Liverpool, worse was to come only days later when Mr Johnson shot off his Mouth again, after it declared that claims it was having an affair with Petronella Wyatt's Ear were 'an inverted pyramid of piffle' a declaration that led to the ground opening beneath it and attempting to swallow it up, while Mr Johnson's pants burst into spontaneous flame. Its reputation in tatters, The Mouth was dismissed from its role, only returning to the Conservative front benches in 2006 as part of new Tory leader David Cameron's assemblage of thrusting and radical old Etonians.

Tired, weary and mentally unbalanced, Mr Johnson shot off his Mouth for the final time when he accused Papua New Guineans of being cannibals. Friends and journalists, hoping for one last misstatement from The Mouth, were gathered at its bedside as it uttered its final words which were 'yoiks', or possibly 'yarroo'. It is to be buried next Saturday, alongside Gogol's Nose and Kafka's Dick.

David Cameron's
Squeaky Clean Image

2005–2007

David Cameron's Squeaky Clean Image inhaled its last breath, exhaled very slowly, said 'Wow!' and expired this weekend following his refusal to deny claims that he smoked cannabis while he was a pupil at Eton 25 years ago.

Dave's Squeaky Clean Image was born in 2005, the offspring of a coterie of Eton chums united by a desire to end the dark days of Michael Howard's leadership which had, strangely, drained the lifeblood of the Tory party. Their far-out plan to fill the vacuum in the centre ground of British politics (left by Labour's sprightly trot to the right under Tony Blair) was initially dismissed as the kind of nonsense dreamed up en route to the all-night garage for a couple of Twix bars and those 'chocolate things with the nuts on them, you know the ones'.

The Squeaky Clean Image was soon sullied during its leadership campaign when it did not deny that it had taken Class A drugs at university, with fellow alumni insisting that it had had 'a normal university experience' – saving money from its grant by buying almost-past-their-sell-by-date goods in the supermarket in order to be able to afford a bag of grass for the weekend which would, inevitably, turn out to be parsley.

Despite this setback The Squeaky Clean Image quickly established itself as a lively presence in British politics, cycling through the streets of West London in vibrant dayglo colours and campaigning for homeowners to erect green windmills on their roof so that we could 'all look at the pretty colours turning in the wind, man'.

But it was The Squeaky Clean Image's adoption of Old Labour policies – most recently the decision to fight the imposition of ID cards – that led critics to suspect that the smoke coming from Conservative Party HQ wasn't the result of Margaret Thatcher spinning rapidly in her grave, but was the natural by-product of the enormous bong the young Tory policy wonks fired up each morning for inspiration.

Despite Tory leaders' traditional association with powerful intoxicants – Winston Churchill lived on a champagne and whisky drip, Margaret Thatcher's 'vitamin injections' kept her in a state of hawk-like readiness for 22 hours a day and Michael Howard never slept at night at all – the hot knives were out. As news of The Squeaky Clean Image's teenage reefer madness was splashed across the front pages of the Sunday newspapers it called for the right to a past that is private, thus immediately promising a future that is far too public for comfort. When Norman Tebbit told Mr Cameron to come clean – in that way only he, and certain black site interrogation operatives, can – The Squeaky Clean Image sniffed its last.

David Cameron's Squeaky Clean Image will be cremated in an environmentally-friendly, and very high Anglican service, at St Withnail's Church of the Camberwell Carrot. There will be a public memorial service, group hug and rave at Glastonbury this summer. It is survived by David Cameron's Youthful Indiscretions.

Faith School Quotas

2006–2006

Many will be saddened to hear of the death of Faith School Quotas, killed whilst travelling in a government vehicle last night.

Born in the early part of 2006, throughout its short life Faith School Quotas upheld a simple creed of religious toleration and understanding, insisting that Faith Schools take up to 25 per cent of their pupils from children of different religious backgrounds or no religious background at all. This creed was based on the, perhaps naive, idea that children whose parents belong to different faith groups should occasionally meet each other and perhaps learn something about each other beyond the fact that they are unbelievers who should be wiped from the face of the earth by a) the forces of righteousness, b) the will of the appropriate God and c) large amounts of explosives.

Tragically, Faith School Quotas died last night, after the government vehicle it was travelling in was involved in a major accident following the decision of its driver, Education Secretary Alan Johnson, to perform a sudden U-turn which resulted in him driving into a sea of religious intolerance. Police are currently interviewing Mr Johnson who it is believed may have been driving whilst intoxicated with the notion of standing for the Labour leadership at the time of the accident.

The funeral will be held on Monday at St Dawkins Church of Unbelief and will be followed by a ceremony of remembrance during which the Archbishop of Canterbury, Cardinal Cormac

Murphy O'Connor, the Chief Rabbi, several imams and a couple of Hare Krishna followers will dance upon the grave. Representatives of the Church of Scientology will be on hand to take a collection, then donate it to themselves.

Faith School Quotas are survived by ghettos, crusades, jihads and Old Firm football matches in Glasgow.

Gordon Brown's Dourness

1994–2007

Gordon Brown's Dourness, the scowl that resided upon the Chancellor's face for so many years, has died, passing away – by some extraordinary cosmic coincidence – at exactly the same time his best friend, Tony Blair, announced his decision to stand down as Labour leader.

Gordon Brown's Dourness was born in 1994 when a perfectly good lunch with Tony Blair at Islington's Granita restaurant left a nasty taste in his mouth. Before that dreadful moment when he nearly choked on his organic glass of water and small piece of stale bread julienne, Gordon had been the life and soul of every Labour Party meeting and late-into-the-night trade union function – entertaining party members and comrades alike with his hilarious impression of Tony Blair impersonating Margaret Thatcher. The meal at Granita at which Tony claimed first dibs on being Labour leader was to change everything – including the political wind – which is why Gordon's face stuck like that for the next decade.

Over the years Gordon Brown's Dourness deepened, particularly when in the company of his best friend Tony Blair. In public it presented an unchanging granite mask to the world and called for 'fiscal prudence', whilst privately hammering on the dividing wall of number 10 in the wee small hours and shouting drunkenly for Tony to 'Give me back my party, you lying, back-stabbing git.' It was when Tony Blair finally set the date for his departure from office that cracks began to appear in the stony visage that had for so long been a gift to Britain's leading impressionists (and Jon Culshaw). By the following day Gordon Brown himself was even overheard cracking a joke ('Knock, Knock, Tony… Who's there…? The removal men… !'). Things went from bad to worse for The Dourness as it suffered the indignity of a new, trendy haircut and, during a walkabout, Gordon Brown was seen cheerily tousling the hair of a small boy – although this was later discovered to be fellow cabinet member Ruth Kelly, who had to go home immediately and whip herself clean.

Even the brief threat of a challenge to Gordon's leadership bid from left-wing Labour MP, John McDonnell, failed to halt the rapid decline of The Dourness (indeed, the comical surprise of discovering that the Labour Party still harboured a left-wing MP left it even more weakened). As Gordon began to skip merrily from press conference to photo opportunity, humming 'This is the Dawning of the Age of Aquarius' and expounding his vision of a new Britain full of eco-towns, LSD on the NHS and tie-dye uniforms for the British Army in Iraq, Gordon Brown's Dourness fell into its last sulk and was no more.

Gordon Brown's Dourness has already been buried in an unmarked grave. During the ceremony close friends and family sang an up-tempo version of 'Dear Prudence' – though best friend, Tony Blair, was unable to attend. Gordon Brown's Dourness is survived by Gordon Brown's Mirth, Gordon Brown's Delight, Gordon Brown's Ecstasy and David Cameron.

The Home Office
1782–2007

The death of The Home Office, following a brutal altercation with a notorious Glaswegian hard man known to gang members as Home Secretary John Reid, will be greeted with shock but little horror by all those who had come to know it.

Born in 1782, the child of the Southern Department and Secretary of State Lord Shelburne (who soon abandoned his progeny for the post of prime minister), from its earliest days The Home Office was at the heart of some of the greatest controversies to afflict the nation. Before it had even learned to crawl it was involved in the most vital affairs of state, including the direction of Crown grants, appointments and preferments (a role which we are advised certainly was not subsequently assigned to Lord Levy or Ruth Turner).

It was only in its fourth decade, however, that The Home Office settled into the job that it was to cleave to for the next 200 years, namely the suppression of the people, which it achieved by suspension of habeas corpus, restrictions on the freedom of assembly and granting its support to such brilliant policing actions as the Peterloo Massacre. It was not long after this that, under the direction of Home Secretary Robert Peel, The Home Office first began to dabble in Class A legislation.

The hard life which The Home Office was to lead (setting up prison hulks, sending felons to Australia, locking up Chartists and general strikers and later even the odd blackshirt), combined with an ever-increasing intake of bills and statutes, began to take its toll. In the mid-1960s, under the influence of Home Secretary Roy 'Flowerchild' Jenkins, The Home Office briefly fell out with 'the Man' and engaged in a series of permissive 'happenings', including relaxation of divorce law and abolition of theatre censorship as well as supporting the legalisation of abortions and homosexuality. This 'fabulous freak out' proved to be merely a mid-life crisis before the inevitable slide into old age.

By the 1980s The Home Office was showing obvious signs of being unable to care for itself. Around the same time it fell under the influence of the first in a sequence of home secretaries addicted to regular injections of publicity (or 'chasing the Murdoch'). Forced to push out more and more laws of lower and lower quality, in recent years The Home Office has shown increasing signs of forgetfulness – often misplacing thousands of prisoners at a time – and paranoia, first insisting on keeping every last citizen under constant CCTV observation, later demanding that each person carry an ID card and be willing to give up their full DNA details to any state employee from a benefits assessor to a lollipop lady. It was in this distracted state that The Home Office first came into contact with John Reid. The tragic result was inevitable.

The Home Office will be buried with little ceremony over the following months. It leaves behind it 24,000 highly dependent civil servants and its two young children, The Ministry of Truth and The Ministry of Love.

Ian Paisley's Refusal to Sit Down

1969–2007

Ian Paisley's Refusal to Sit Down lost its long and extremely loud battle against gravity yesterday when Unionist leader Ian Paisley agreed to sit down with his arch-enemy, Sinn Fein leader Gerry Adams – the two men having reached a historic agreement to share power in Northern Ireland rather than continue the squabble over who has the most right to the Six Counties… I mean Ulster… or Londonderry… I mean Derry…

Ian Paisley's Refusal to Sit Down took its first faltering steps in 1969 in protest at the British Army being sent into the province to protect Catholics from Loyalist attacks. Prior to that date, of course, there had been no sectarian divide in Northern Ireland, no one had ever heard of the Battle of the Boyne or seen an Orange Man and Catholics and Protestants skipped hand-in-hand through the Six Counties singing 'All You Need Is Love'.

But as the oh-so-slightly-euphemistically-titled The Troubles began to wreak havoc across the province, Ian Paisley's Refusal to Sit Down made him very popular on buses full of (Protestant) pensioners and pregnant (Protestant) women, but caused him great personal anguish as, year after year, it stopped him from winning the much-coveted Belfast Apprentice Boys' Musical Chairs Contest.

Throughout the 1970s and 1980s, The Refusal grew in strength (and volume) – refusing to bend at the knee for anyone, or indeed apply the prescribed ointment to the appropriate area. In the late 1990s, when Tony Blair encouraged both sides to replace stand-up rows with stand-up talks, agreements were made which led to the decommissioning of James Nesbitt, Gloria Hunniford and Tom Paulin – making sure that they could never again be used to terrorise innocent civilians in the province or on the mainland.

But having stood up for nearly forty years, The Refusal was getting tired, and as Northern Ireland Secretary, Peter Hain, threatened to dissolve the Stormont Assembly, it was on its last legs. Ian Paisley's Refusal to Sit Down finally buckled and fell into the waiting arms of Gerry Adams... and onto a large rubber ring.

The Refusal is predeceased by Northern Ireland's vital bowler hat and ski-mask industries and by the painters of sectarian murals. It will be buried at Stormont tonight once General John de Chastelain has confirmed that Ian Paisley's Refusal to Sit Down has been interred and 'put beyond use'.

The Refusal is survived by Ian Paisley's Mouth, Gerry Adams' Beard and Britain's fabulous history of partition which has successfully kept the peace for so many years between Israel and Palestine, Pakistan and India, the Republic and Northern Ireland and numbers 10 and 11 Downing Street.

John Reid's Sense of Shame

1947–2006

It is with enormous regret that *As a Dodo* must announce the death of Home Secretary John Reid's Sense of Shame, struck down during an appearance by Mr Reid before inmates at Wormwood Scrubs Prison. While sources at the Home Office insist that The Sense of Shame had been discharging its duties in the normal way, friends and colleagues say it had long been showing signs of stress and overwork.

Born in North Lanarkshire just after World War Two and educated at St Patrick's High School in Coatbridge, John Reid's Sense of Shame was a vigorous youth, well equipped for coping with a lad whose gentle manner and calm tones put the fear of God into all who dared to cross his path, whether he was contemplating demanding dinner money from his teachers or threatening to report fellow ten-year-olds for hanging around with children near the school gates.

The Sense of Shame was at Reid's side throughout his education, accompanying him during his PhD in economic history and further postgraduate studies in low-level political bruising and demagoguery as a member of the Communist Party of Great Britain. With Reid's entry into the Labour Party and Parliament, cracks in his relationship with The Sense of Shame started to show. Difficulties began in the mid-1990s when Reid, keen for advancement, began to throw aside all his ideological baggage in order to join the vanguard of New Labour. Matters worsened as Reid, desperate to advance, repeatedly used tabloid headlines to fuel his increasing need for red top. As Health Secretary and Defence Secretary he was able, with The Sense's help, to manage his cravings to a certain degree, but with his appointment as Home Secretary his need to 'chase the Murdoch' overpowered him. Soon he was spending most of his days in the gutter press, eager to menace a minority or beat up a judge for the price of one more hit – all the while blaming his troubles on civil servants, social workers and Jeremy Paxman.

Strained almost to breaking point, The Sense did all it could to save the home secretary from the pit of addiction, but to no avail, as Reid accused the House of Lords of pandering to paedophiles before making his way to Wormwood Scrubs. There, to the delight of assembled hacks and the bemusement of inmates, Reid launched into a performance of the dance of the veiled threats, blaming violent crime on Tory leader David Cameron, the probation service, Jack Straw, David Blunkett, Charles Clarke and anybody whose name wasn't John Reid. It was as The Sense rushed up to stop him that Reid chose to assault his oldest friend, delivering the headbutt that would ultimately deliver it to the grave. Police were called to the scene but failed to arrive until long after the (frequent) offender had made off.

John Reid's Sense of Shame will be buried hastily and without ceremony. It is survived by reduced civil liberties and tabloid hysteria.

Labour Party Finances
1900–2006

Labour Party Finances expired today after creditors decided to call in loans of £23.4 million. It had been poorly for some time with doctors saying it had had a 'difficult financial year'.

Born on 27 February 1900 following the marriage of the Trades Union Congress and the Fabian Society, Labour Party Finances earned its keep by winning numerous beautiful baby contests – mostly in the industrial districts of the north of England, the Midlands, Scotland and Wales – and, at the tender age of 23, it hit the jackpot when it won its first national popularity contest.

Following Labour's landslide election victory in 1945, The Finances became so cash-rich Labour was able to give vast sums of money back to ordinary voters by nationalising electricity, gas, the railways and the iron, steel and coal industries. In 1948 millions of Britons benefited from a massive dividend on their taxes with the introduction of the welfare state.

The Finances went from strength to strength in the 1960s with the nationalisation of The Beatles, which allowed every teenage girl in the country the chance to own a piece of a moptop – normally a lock of hair or a piece of a collarless suit torn off Paul McCartney. But despite this boost, Harold Wilson lost millions of pounds of taxpayers' money on Tony Benn's disastrous concept album, *Lucy in the Sky with Keynesian Economics*, and had to devalue the pound.

However, following James Callaghan's refusal to pay the binmen's Christmas box in 1978 and the infamous Winter of Discontent that resulted, financial ruin was to fall on Labour Party Finances when it lost its job in 1979 and was forced to sign on at the DHSS.

For the next 18 years, Labour Party Finances failed to find gainful employment. Reduced to watching daytime television and fulminating against the Conservatives as they financed the nation by selling off electricity, gas, the railways, and the iron, steel and coal industries, The Finances only managed to claw its way out of debt in 1997 by promising to sell off anything else that wasn't nailed down.

Sadly, the long spell on the dole had done severe damage and The Finances was forced into selling first its principles, then offering private finance initiatives, NHS hospitals, foundation schools and peerages at knock-down prices. In the end, the decision to consolidate all The Finances debts into 'one, easy-to-manage debt' was the final nail in the coffin as, in April 2006, the Fraud Squad launched an investigation. Choked by an extensive paper trail and a number of irate men who had been refused a peerage, Labour Party Finances finally gave up the ghost and passed away surrounded by close friends and family including Richard Branson, Rupert Murdoch and Steptoe and Son.

Labour Party Finances will be buried in a pauper's grave at St Vorderman's Church of the Receivers and is survived by Conservative Party Debts of £35.3 million. Well-wishers and anyone who likes the smooth feel of ermine against their skin are requested to send cash in used notes.

The Liberal Democrats' Drink Problem

1999–2006

The Liberal Democrats, along with many members of the British press, have today been remembering the party's Drink Problem after news of the Lib. Dem.'s attempts to bury it in secret were leaked to journalists at *The Times*.

The Liberal Democrats' Drink Problem was born in 1999, when TV chat show guest, bon viveur and occasional MP Charles Kennedy announced his intention to stand for the party leadership, something he achieved with the aid of a skilled campaign team, a set of exciting policies and a handy wall to prop himself up against. While at first it confined itself to private appearances and occasional performances for friends in the bars of the House of Commons, by late 2002 The Drink Problem decided it was time to bring itself to the public's attention, starring in a performance of *Whisky Galore*, with Jeremy Paxman playing the stuffy and overbearing head of the local militia. Its appetite for the public stage whetted, The Drink Problem was soon a regular on the political circuit. In early 2003 it brought the house down with several performances of *The Man Who Wasn't There* during prime minister's questions.

By the run up to the general election The Drink Problem was successfully reprising Bob Hope's role as an inept man completely out of his depth, playing

the eponymous hero of *The Paleface*. By late 2005, however, The Drink Problem was losing its popularity with party and public. Soon it was appearing to small crowds of the elderly and infirm at assorted seaside venues and any other places where Liberal Democrat conferences were being held.

The Liberal Democrats eventually buried their Drink Problem in an extremely private ceremony held on a patch of waste ground in the early hours of the morning. At the head of the mourners was party leader Sir Menzies Campbell, who performed his task of keeping an eye out for any possible witnesses with his customary dignity and aplomb. The burial, illuminated by moonlight and Simon Hughes's battery-operated torch, was marred only by the need to keep absolutely quiet to avoid attracting anyone's attention and by Charles Kennedy making several attempts to climb out of the coffin and get to the bar before last orders.

The Liberal Democrats' Drink Problem is survived by countless empty whisky bottles and several distraught distilleries.

Loans for Peerages

2005–2007

Loans for Peerages – the modern, democratic method by which our unelected rulers are appointed to the House of Lords – was found dead this week shortly after Tony Blair was questioned for a second time by the Metropolitan Police. Sources indicate that foul play is suspected.

Born just before the general election in 2005, Loans for Peerages was the child of Labour's desperate need to prop up its ailing finances and an antiquated system of appointing anyone with a spare million to the unelected upper chamber of the Palace of Westminster.

It proved to be a popular baby: within days of its birth it was attracting unprecedented media attention as it crawled, literally, from boardroom to boardroom soliciting 'loans' at a rate of interest not seen in your high street building society since your manager got high on genuine Albanian champagne-style fizz at the last Christmas party and opened the vaults saying, 'Take whatever you want.' Within only two years, however, it was causing controversy, with Scotland Yard detectives forced to step in after complaints that it had committed offences under the Honours (Prevention of Abuses) Act of 1925 when some lenders alleged that they hadn't received their ermine-collared free gifts.

The death of Loans for Peerages was first, mistakenly, reported in 2006, following claims that it had been fatally wounded by the arrest of Labour's chief fundraiser, Lord Levy, and the questioning under caution of MPs and officials from Labour and other parties. The reports turned out to be false when it was revealed early in 2007 that, far from being dead, Loans for Peerages had merely been swept under the nearest available piece of carpet.

Loans for Peerages' resurrection was to prove brief as its demise was quickened by the arrest of Mr Blair's 'gatekeeper', Director of Government Relations Ruth Turner, and the re-arrest of Lord Levy on suspicion of perverting the course of justice, not forgetting a further police interview with Tony Blair himself, who is believed to have explained that he saw nothing of Loans for Peerages at all as he was tying his shoelaces at the time.

Loans for Peerages was buried by the highest bidder at the Church of *Deal or No Deal*. Following a brief sermon by the Reverend David Lloyd George, the collection trough was passed, a deeply emotional eulogy was read by several very rich men who mourned their chances of ever becoming peers by the back door, and a choir of businessmen sang hymn number 427 'What a Friend We Have in Tony'.

Loans for Peerages is survived by a discredited government and a quasi-mediaeval system of patronage.

Tony Blair's Green Credentials

1994–2007

Tony Blair's Green Credentials have been emptied into the wormery by his own sustainable development adviser, Jonathon Porritt, after losing a long battle with plausibility.

Tony Blair's Green Credentials were born in July 1994 when he became leader of the Labour Party and immediately began throwing out old Labour policies harmful to the chances of Tony Blair ever becoming prime minister. Clause IV – the party's commitment to the common ownership of the means of production, distribution and exchange – was replaced with more Blair-friendly values such as unbridled consumerism, private finance initiatives and massive 'loans' from lenders who would mysteriously became peers soon after bunging Labour the cash, along with a new emphasis on sounding caring about the environment while actually doing bugger all about it.

With New Labour's election victory in May 1997 Tony Blair's Green Credentials were firmly ensconced at number 10 – behind a desk made from timber taken from a renewable source, and in an office powered solely by the sun shining out of Mr Blair's backside.

Tony Blair's Green Credentials made their mark on the map by instigating a widespread plan to reduce governmental waste by recycling old Conservative policies such as privatising national assets, mucking up education and the NHS, appointing Home Secretaries who apparently base their moral philosophy on Genghis Khan and allowing cabinet ministers to become embroiled in embarrassing personal and financial scandals.

The unwavering pursuit of the eco-friendly even extended beyond Britain's borders when, despite evidence to the contrary, Tony Blair's Green Credentials refused to create new foreign policies, instead using second-hand American policies on waste disposal – largely involving the transportation of metals, explosives and depleted uranium to the Middle East where they were used to recycle buildings into rubble and people into body bags.

Sadly the continuing uncontrolled noxious emissions from cabinet ministers – particularly John Reid, David Milliband and Ruth Kelly – sounded the death knell for Tony Blair's Green Credentials. When Mr Blair himself refused to accept the disastrous consequences of long-haul flights for the environment, or the unacceptable size of the scandal footprint left by his free holidays at the homes of bland UK pop stars, The Credentials slipped into a coma before being pronounced dead by green activists and Mr Blair's own environment minister.

The service for Tony Blair's Green Credentials will be conducted at St Sellafield's Holy Roman Reprocessing Plant before being leaked into the Irish Sea.

Tony Blair's Green Credentials are survived by David Cameron's Solar-powered, Hydro-electric Windmill and Sir Menzies Campbell's Extraordinary Conservation of Energy.

Tony Blair's Premiership
1997–2007

The streets of Britain were today filled with weeping hordes as a great portion of humanity gathered to greet the passing of Tony Blair's Premiership with tears of unalloyed joy.

The Premiership was born on 2 May 1997. Like the Roman people, exhausted by the cruel and incompetent rule of Tiberius, gleefully saluting their new emperor Caligula, so the British people, exhausted by the cruelty of the Thatcherites and incompetence of the Majorites, gleefully saluted their new prime minister as, flanked by his loyal Praetorian guard of spin doctors, he swept into number 10 Downing Street.

Young and bold, The Premiership moved with a reckless pace, acting swiftly on its greatest priorities, encouraging the party to cast aside all that it once believed in, whether it be promises to raise income tax and restore trade union rights, pledges to pursue nuclear disarmament or even its long-held commitment to socialism.

Though briefly distracted by the need to produce the appropriate strained expression and catch in the voice around the time of the death of Diana, Princess of Wales, The Premiership soon embarked on a series of wide-ranging reforms, introducing devolution, removing peers from the House of Lords, passing the Freedom of Information Act, creating the post of Mayor of London and evicting Downing Street cat Humphrey from its long-time home for fear of aggravating Cherie's allergies. All were hailed as great successes. Unfortunately The Premiership itself was later to regret each and every one of them. Happily, The Premiership had other strings to its bow. Unhappily one of them was the Millennium Dome, a folly which sought to commemorate the past thousand years by putting a big tent on some disused wasteland and filling it with exhibits so staggeringly tacky they could have been 'lovingly handcrafted' for the Franklin Mint.

By the end of its first term, however, The Premiership was able to boast one unalloyed success: the Northern Irish peace process. At last there was an achievement Mr Blair felt able to call completely his own, despite the fact much of the spade work had actually been done by John Major. Buoyed by this knowledge, the memory of the dark days under Mr Major and housing prices rising faster than a city trader's bonus, Tony Blair's Premiership was swept back to power in 2001.

Having already discovered the enormous kudos that could be won by blowing places up following his intervention in the Yugoslav conflict, Mr Blair was delighted to find that the new President of the US was intent on destabilising as much of the globe as possible, by tearing up any treaties he could find and sending troops to anywhere Dick Cheney felt Halliburton could secure lucrative reconstruction contracts. The Iraq War gave Mr Blair the opportunity to pose with tanks and try to sound Churchillian and – thanks to the hatred and suspicion it stirred up – also gave him the opportunity to pass increasingly repressive legislation to issue teenagers, pensioners and everyone in between with ASBOs, instant fines, and detention without charge.

Despite all this and more (top-up fees, the David Kelly affair, foundation hospitals to name just a few) The Premiership somehow succeeded in returning to power in 2005. However, none who looked upon it could doubt that it was wounded, even as they noted that the majority of the wounds were self-inflicted. Worse was yet to come when it became clear that, in accordance with immemorial practice, the government had been merrily sending major party donors towards the ermine outfitters and seats in the House of Lords with all the speed and urgency normally associated with one's bladder suddenly realising that it contains eight pints of Special Brew and it's a long journey to the lavatories. Thus it was that The Premiership saw Mr Blair become the first prime minister to be interviewed by police whilst in office, even as eternal rival Gordon Brown at last plucked up the courage to insist that Mr Blair do the decent thing and fall upon the sword Gordon had helpfully placed between Tony's shoulder blades.

So it was that Tony Blair's Premiership passed on to a better world – having left a much worse one behind. It was buried at St Gordon's Church of the Best Served Cold alongside the corpse of its (sometimes) faithful pet bulldog, John Prescott. It is survived by Mr Blair's new role as Special Ironic Envoy to the Middle East.

Celebrity

Britney Spears's Hair

1981–2007

Britney Spears's Hair died this weekend after it was forcibly removed from its life support system in a Los Angeles tattoo parlour. It had been unwell for some time as a result of obsessive interest in its every move, flick, wave and tint from people around the world who deemed knowledge of The Hair more important than an understanding of history, science, politics or even themselves.

Britney Spears's Hair was born in 1981 to Britney Spears herself and led a normal and unremarkable life – barring a childish experimentation with Mickey Mouse ears – until 1998 when it found itself propelled against its will into the paparazzi flashlights following the success of Britney's debut album, *Baby One More Time*.

Almost overnight The Hair became the most photographed celebrity in the world, replacing Jordan's cleavage and Tony Blair's cheekily self-satisfied grin as the holy grail of snapshots.

Where once The Hair had been able to spend its days sensibly brushed and parted or even matted and hidden under a hat if it so wished, now The Hair faced a daily barrage of media speculation about its next reinvention and endless questions about everything from its favourite conditioner to its thoughts on the Middle East peace process.

Despite its astonishing financial success, The Hair's behaviour became increasingly erratic as it was hounded from nightclub to wedding chapel to divorce court. In a desperate bid to return to a more simple style, The Hair checked itself into rehab for a quick rinse and blow-dry but checked itself out before completing the treatment, resulting in a tonsorial disaster that pushed the war in Iraq off the front pages.

The damage had been done and Britney Spears filed for divorce from The Hair citing irreconcilable artistic differences, although she was present as the two parted company and The Hair was finally allowed to rest in peace, beneath the barber's chair, before being swept away for the final time.

Britney Spears's Hair will be buried at the St Samson Church of Non-Denominational Celebrity Hair, Hollywood, in a private service attended by friends, family, minders, paparazzi and hundreds of thousands of distraught fans before The Hair is exhumed by bald acolytes and sold on eBay.

Britney Spears's Hair was predeceased by William Shatner's Thatch and Demi Moore's Locks. It is survived by tabloid editors tearing their hair out as they while away the time until they can print the next Britney up-skirt crotch shot without more than the usual amount of hypocrisy.

Celebrity Big Brother

2001–2007

Celebrity Big Brother's place in the nation's affections died this week, live on national television, following a massive public protest against the bullying of Bollywood superstar Shilpa Shetty by the trio of luminaries that is Jade Goody (reality TV show loser), Danielle Lloyd (second string glamour model and footballer's girlfriend) and Jo O'Meara (dog breeder and former S Club 7 member).

Born in 2001, *Celebrity Big Brother* was the fruit of an unholy attempt to meddle with nature by knitting together the lowest forms of reality TV – with a collection of talentless Z-listers, has-beens and sociopaths... and Jack Dee – to create a monster capable of ~~milking credulous couch potatoes~~ entertaining the British public.

Over the next seven years, *Celebrity Big Brother* was to corral a series of increasingly desperate and publicity-hungry non-entities in its televisual zoo in a horrendous spectacle not seen since the closure of the public gallery of Bedlam. So-called celebrities such as Les Dennis, Germaine Greer, Michael Barrymore and George Galloway eagerly debased themselves on national television in a desperate bid to boost their public appeal. Sadly for anyone with faith in the British public, the plan succeeded.

It was with this year's crop of intellectual heavyweights and entertainment superstars that the programme reached an all-time low as producers signed up Jade Goody: a woman whose fame is based on the solid foundation of not knowing the location of 'East Angular', national guilt brought on by a campaign of tabloid vilification and the failure to win a past series of *Big Brother*. Faced with the psychological torture of being placed in close proximity to a woman from another country with a posh-sounding accent and the ability to string two words together without either of them being an Anglo-Saxon monosyllable, Ms Goody, along with acolytes Ms Lloyd and Ms O'Meara, was understandably left with no choice but to resort to a campaign of petty-minded and foul mouthed-abuse unworthy of a playground spat.

The ailing programme's demise came with the decision of sponsor Carphone Warehouse to withdraw Channel 4's vital supply of sponsorship cash after a suggestion that the company change it's name to Freakshow Warehouse failed to win favour.

News of the programme's demise was greeted with enormous sadness by those lined up to take part in the next programme, believed to include Jim Davidson, Bernard Manning and Adolf Hitler. *Celebrity Big Brother* is survived by Channel 4's premium rate eviction line, Endemol's enormous bank balance and the worst period in Anglo-Indian relations since the Raj.

Cherie Blair's WAGhood

1997–2006

The news that Cherie Blair's time as a leading member of the England WAGs (Wives And Girlfriends) has passed away after nine-and-a-half years has come as an enormous shock to expensive hairdressers and style consultants across Britain and an enormous relief to Labour Party supporters and Downing Street officials.

Cherie Blair's WAGhood was born in May 1997 when, with her husband elevated to the premiership, humble Cherie Blair – the straightforward young woman who once told a reporter she could have grown up to be a simple Liverpudlian shop girl – joined the ranks of 'Wives And Girlfriends' of the international scene's most famous players.

As a WAG Cherie brought something unique to the celebrity firmament, even if that unique something was merely a tendency to shoot her mouth off at extremely unfortunate moments. Certainly, things began well for Cherie's WAGhood – with her husband's electrifying pace of reform and exquisite bill-passing skills receiving praise abroad as well as at home, Mrs Blair soon found herself jetting first class around the globe, staying in the most luxurious locations and being pictured in the most glamorous nightspots in the most expensive of designer creations.

While Tony spent his days juggling balls with top-flight international players such as Silvio 'I Own the Referee' Berlusconi and George 'Bomb Your Legs Off' Bush, Cherie spent them indulging her hobby of being a lawyer, giggling with her style consultants and £275-a-go hairdressers, or taking house-buying trips with Australian conmen. Her evenings were spent on Tony's arm, wining and dining with the country's leading celebrities, actors, artists, pop stars and also Sir Cliff Richard.

It may be trite to assert that such a blessed life could not be long-lived but it was nonetheless true. As the years passed, and Mr Blair's popularity waned, Cherie found herself facing the prospect of her WAGhood being relegated to the bench. Attempts to carve out a career in charity work were frustrated by the fact a major beneficiary so often seemed to be Cherie herself, while attempts to carve out a career as a respected judge were frustrated by her tendency to indulge in Mayan rebirthing ceremonies to readjust her energy flow. The final blow came when Tony suffered a dreadful injury following a tackle from behind by several members of his own team, led by Gordon Brown. Facing isolation and loss of her WAG privileges, Cherie's WAGhood spontaneously combusted.

The funeral ceremony was held in Manchester on Tuesday. As The WAGhood's small urn was placed in its niche before an honour guard of Hopi ear candle sellers and an audience who had been forced to pay £300 a head for the privilege of attending, Cherie herself was overcome by her emotions. That these emotions were chiefly malice and rage became evident as she had to be dragged from the graveside, screaming 'F★★★ing Brown. I'll rip the lying Scottish get's f★★★ing throat out'.

Cherie Blair's WAGhood is survived by a massive mortgage, a series of highly profitable 'charity' lectures and Sarah Brown.

The Death of Diana, Princess of Wales

1997–2006

A grieving nation woke this morning to the news that The Death of Diana, Princess of Wales – which has exercised bloggers, newspaper columnists and other members of the personality-disordered classes for the last nine years – has died. According to police accounts, The Death was being driven at speed by an Egyptian man drunk on money when it ran completely out of control and crashed into Lord Steven's inquiry into the circumstances of the late ex-royal's death.

The Death of Diana first came to prominence in 1997 when the ex-wife of heir-to-the-throne and pontificator-in-chief Prince Charles was transformed overnight from a good-looking, rather dim, mother of two and the subject of salacious tabloid gossip and innuendo-laden jokes into a saintly figure of surpassing goodness and victim of an uncaring world by the combination of a tragic accident and a mawkish media. It reached its apotheosis only weeks later when the late princess was buried in a sea of hypocrisy and appalling Elton John singles by millions of people, all of whom claimed to have some deep personal connection with Diana, despite never having come within a paparazzo's focal-length of her.

Only days after the funeral, members of the police were called to the burial site where they discovered that The Death of Diana had been removed from its grave by a group of men described by witnesses as a 'bunch of Internet nutters, desperate tabloid editors and Mohamed Al Fayed'. The men are understood to have taken the corpse to a laboratory at the *Daily Express* where they strove desperately to resurrect The Death by injecting it with front page headlines and a series of incredible conspiracy theories involving the British security services and the Duke of Edinburgh, including the extraordinary suggestion that both parties are capable of performing anything beyond basic bodily functions with sufficient competence to deceive the world's media.

Despite their best efforts, The Death of Diana was simply unable to survive in a world where the French police, the British police, a British coroner, Lord Stevens and anyone with a more than passing acquaintance with reality could find no evidence to support a conspiracy theory.

The Death was buried on Thursday morning in a moving state ceremony alongside several pieces of bad news for the British government, including the decision to drop the SFO inquiry into the Al Yamamah arms deal , the axing of thousands of rural post offices and the questioning of Tony Blair by police in relation to the cash for peerages affair.

The Death of Diana was mourned by Mohamed Al Fayed, the *Daily Express*, Elton John and millions of people who should really find more important things to fill their lives. The Death of Diana is survived by the Death of JFK, the Death of Elvis and the Death of Sanity.

Jeremy Clarkson

1960–2006

We at As a Dodo *must apologise for the following – wholly inaccurate – obituary for Mr Jeremy Clarkson, who is (we are assured both by his friends and his inescapable presence on TV, radio and in print) still, in fact, alive. We can only blame this egregious error on a) our own incompetence and b) the petty jealousy of the member of staff engaged to write the piece.*

It is difficult to relay the impact that the sudden and unexpected death of journalist, broadcaster, motoring expert and professional loud-mouthed know-it-all Jeremy Clarkson will have upon the world.

Jeremy Charles Robert Clarkson was born in 1960 to a long line of Yorkshiremen and exhibited the virtues of his home county, namely forthrightness and plain-speaking (or 'being loud' and 'being rude' as they are known outside Yorkshire). He learnt the craft that was to bring him fame as a child when – allowed into the pub to collect the crisps and Coca-Cola he would be imbibing in the family car while his parents chatted with friends in the snug – he spotted his first pub know-it-all, holding forth at length on why Richard Nixon would beat Leonid Brezhnev in a fight and how all Italians smelled suspiciously of garlic. As he watched the frankly terrified expressions on the faces of the know-it-all's audience, Clarkson knew he had found his ideal job.

After spending many a night hunched under his bedcovers with *The Big Boy's Book of Facts* and *The Hitler Youth Guide to Everything* (not to mention several mysteriously soiled copies of *Health and*

Efficiency) young Jeremy was ready to find the perfect tool to display his burgeoning skills. After realising that the perfect tool was himself, he went on to search for the arena in which to express his art and was soon to find himself among the tedious, mileage-and-torque-obsessed men of motoring journalism. With his ability to deliver outrageous and ill-thought-through opinions by means of heavily-prepared and overwrought metaphors, Clarkson soon found himself promoted to television where he became a hugely successful presenter of the BBC's *Top Gear* programme and a hugely less successful presenter of the chat show *Clarkson*.

Friends believe Mr Clarkson was deeply affected by his friend and co-presenter Richard Hammond's recent, appalling, high-speed accident and – unable to cope with being second best in any area – was driven to outdo Mr Hammond's near-death experience by going 'just that little bit further'. This, at least, is the only reasonable explanation anyone can come up with for his decision to break into Her Majesty's Naval Base Clyde, Faslane – aided only by a BBC camera crew, a large collection of over-extended similes and extensive gurning to camera – and smuggle himself aboard nuclear submarine HMS Vanguard. Once inside the sub, Mr Clarkson strapped himself to a Trident nuclear missile and – having acquired the launch codes from a senior Naval official after reducing him to a quivering wreck with a three-hour tirade on the obnoxiousness of the French – launched himself at the nearest Greenpeace headquarters with a cry of 'Eat atomic death, tree-huggers', and a few pithy remarks about the lack of leather or walnut trim on the latest inter-continental ballistic missiles. As a result of his actions, it is understood several of Mr Clarkson's remaining atoms now hold the British water, air and land speed records.

Jeremy Clarkson is survived by a long-suffering family and a note reading 'In your face, Hammond.'

London's Glittering West End

1663–2006

Doctors at St Luvvie's Hospital have confirmed that London's Glittering West End, known to friends as Theatreland, passed away this evening after being cruelly choked to death by a surfeit of film-to-stage transfers, musicals based on the back catalogues of 1970s pop groups and Andrew Lloyd Webber.

Born in the aftermath of the Restoration to a fun-loving King Charles II, several playwrights and a large number of extremely willing actresses, London's Glittering West End soon developed into the theatrical centre of Britain... as well as the scene of many encounters between the aforementioned fun-loving king and willing actresses.

Over the coming years Theatreland was to play host to a varied and astounding range of work from playwrights including Shakespeare, Shaw, Ibsen, Molière, Pinter, Priestley and Beckett, and performances from such notables as Nell Gwynn, David Garrick, Sarah Bernhardt, Henry Irving, Laurence Olivier, Judi Dench, Peter O'Toole and several productions of Sir John Gielgud's Hamlet in local lavatory cubicles.

Despite its success, the years did not weigh easily on the West End. As time passed it began to suffer the inevitable ailments of age, its heart increasingly affected by fatty deposits of musical theatre. By the 1990s friends began to note that Theatreland's ability to keep up with current events was failing. Increasingly a shadow of its former self, London's Glittering West End became content to sit back and rock gently to the unthreatening strains of 1970s pop groups such as ABBA and Queen and ever more reliant on a diet of pre-digested *Lion Kings*, *Producers* and other film-to-stage transfers. Unable even to feed itself properly, it was eventually found choking on a mashed-up production of *Dirty Dancing*.

The funeral of London's Glittering West End will be attended by Andrew Lloyd Webber, Ben Elton and several coach parties of confused pensioners under the impression they are at a performance of *Les Misérables*. Presiding vicar Cameron Mackintosh has confirmed that the ceremony will be in the best possible taste, the coffin being slowly lowered into its grave accompanied by a roller-skating tap routine and Michael Ball's rendition of Boney M's 'Ra-Ra-Rasputin'. The final burial of The West End will take place on Friday, although doctors expect it to be revived in about twenty years time in a wave of ridiculous nostalgia for the noughties.

London's Glittering West End is survived by *Andrew Lloyd Webber, The Musical!* (book by Ben Elton, lyrics by Tim Rice and music by Puccini).

Paul Burrell's Link to Reality

1958–2006

Doctors at the St Diana Hospital for the Self-Deluded have confirmed that former Royal Butler Paul Burrell's Link to Reality passed away this week. Although reports from the hospital remain unclear, it appears that The Link – which had been in poor health for many years – entered a coma early on Sunday after a brief, 17-hour, chat with Mr Burrell himself about the former butler's deep and abiding love for Diana, Princess of Wales, and how much he meant to her.

The product of a childhood in a coal-mining village in the north of England, The Link spent much of its troubled life in Mr Burrell's company. When he first joined the royal staff, The Link decided to go with him, taking it upon itself to listen to young Paul's tales of royal goings-on while quietly reminding him of his position – at that time third under-footstool-in-waiting.

The relationship between the pair became more difficult in 1987, when Mr Burrell was appointed butler to the Prince and Princess of Wales. With Mr Burrell spending much of his time in the glare of the media spotlight (even if only at the very edge of that glare and usually concealed beneath the princess's shopping), The Link found itself seeing less and less of its old friend. Things worsened still following the royal divorce when – apparently prompted by an offhand remark from Diana – Mr Burrell spent several months believing he was a rock.

Following Diana's death, The Link's attempts to see Mr Burrell became ever more infrequent. Soon it became content to sit at home, watching its old friend as he chose to maintain a quiet and dignified silence by selling his story to the world and eating kangaroo testicles on ITV 'reality' programme *I'm A Nonentity, Get Me Out of Here*.

Soon The Link's health began to fail, even as Mr Burrell was finding a new role for himself as keeper of a private museum containing a surprisingly large assortment of Diana's property and as defender of the princess's reputation against all those who might wish to do her wrong, such as her own children.

The Link is survived by the only person on this earth who ever really knew and understood Diana.

Prince Harry's Bad Boy Reputation

2002–2007

Buckingham Palace insiders and Ministry of Defence officials have today confirmed to a shocked nation that The 'Bad Boy' Reputation of third in line to the British throne Prince Harry has passed away, replaced in its prime by the heroic reputation of plain 'Cornet Wales'(not, as some had assumed, a Duchy Organic ice cream flavour, but rather the title the Prince will bear during his military service in Iraq as a member of the Blues and Royals Regiment).

Prince Harry's Bad Boy Reputation was born in 2002. Like so many bad boys, Prince Harry earned his reputation after years of living off the state and wandering around aimlessly on vast estates. Though admittedly the estates Harry wandered around had much better grouse shooting than the average inner-city tower block, the Prince nonetheless followed the path of many a bored British teen and began drinking heavily and smoking cannabis. Relatives feared these habits might go from bad to worse, leading to addiction to hard drugs or even dabbling with a Conservative Party leadership bid.

Despite the Prince's antics having landed him on the front page of every British tabloid, there were soon concerns for his newborn Bad Boy Reputation when it was announced that he would be attending a drug counselling centre for a day. Much to the consternation of all those – chiefly newspaper editors – who cared about The Reputation, Harry soon seemed to have turned his back on his rebellious ways and learned to follow more traditional royal standards of behaviour, falling off polo ponies and calling his French chef a 'F★★★ing Frog'.

Happily for all concerned, Harry was soon back on form again and by 2005 he was partying the nights away in West End nightclubs and engaging in drunken scuffles with members of the paparazzi.

In the same year the Prince entered the Royal Military Academy Sandhurst, intent on becoming a cavalry officer despite warnings that he was obviously overqualified for such a post, being in possession of a chin. Those who feared that pulling on the uniform his ancestors had worn with pride might prove a fatal blow to his Bad Boy Reputation were proved wrong when the uniform in question turned out to be that of a Schutzstaffel Oberführer.

Despite such positive signs, Prince Harry's Bad Boy Reputation slipped away this week following the announcement that the Prince is to lead a troop of 12 men in Iraq. The Reputation will be buried with full military honours and an item of fruit inserted in its rear after a street brawl outside a Mayfair nightspot. It is survived by acres of newsprint praising Harry as a modern-day Achilles and the only 12 British soldiers in Iraq who can be absolutely confident of having all the latest military equipment (boots, body armour, working guns) and backup they could ever want.

Prince Harry's Bad Boy Reputation
2002–2007: A Correction

We at *As a Dodo* Towers wish to apologise to our readers for ~~yet another massive cock-up~~ serious errors in our obituary for Prince Harry's Bad Boy Reputation. We have been contacted by officials at Clarence House who have asked us to note that senior army officers have now realised that it is entirely possible that as a) a soldier in the British army and b) in all probability the son of the heir to the throne, there is some slight chance of the young Prince being targeted by those opposing the British and American presence in Iraq. Indeed, we further understand from reports in the British press (apparently based on a conversation with someone in the pub, who knows a bloke who knows a bloke who once read Andy McNab's *Bravo Two Zero*) that orders have already been issued to an unidentified (and almost certainly fictional) sniper to regard Prince Harry as his sole target. In the circumstances we have been asked to point out that Prince Harry will not now be joining his regiment in Iraq and, accordingly, his Bad Boy Reputation will, far from being dead, continue to embarrass the royal family for years to come.

Prince William and Kate Middleton's Relationship

2003–2007

Prince William and Kate Middleton's Relationship – a four-year-long courtship consisting of vacuous polo matches and tedious skiing holidays – has breathed its last after being suffocated by a media desperate for a union as exciting and newsworthy as Charles and Diana or Andrew and Fergie, or even Edward and Sophie.

The Relationship began when William and Kate first met – like so many couples – at university. The humdrum circumstances of The Relationship's conception – Kate and Will's eyes having met over a supper of baked beans on toast in their shared student home (excitedly reported in *The Sun* under the headline 'House of Wind-sor!') – did not deter the journalists and paparazzi fighting to capture every second of the couple's time together as they sauntered to the local Co-op to buy another bottle of economy washing-up liquid or shared a pint of lager shandy over the course of a whole evening whilst discussing the plot of *Hollyoaks*.

Consisting as it did of long hours of the couple bemusedly poring over text books in the library or doing their laundry (daringly, without the aid of a valet) and despite being even less interesting than the members of David Cameron's shadow cabinet (excluding Boris Johnson), The Relationship was nonetheless dogged by reporters at every step. So it was that William's decision to abandon the notoriously difficult (for a royal) History of Art course in favour of crushingly boring Geography was greeted with front page headlines – 'Wills Gives Art Elbow!', 'Nudesflash!' but an almost complete lack of interest from the public.

Regularly outshone by the antics of his brother Harry, William obediently joined the army, where he tragically failed to get off his head on drugs, dress up in a Nazi uniform or even blearily chat up a barmaid in his local pub. The press were left able merely to hail the young Prince as the potential saviour of democracy in Iraq and healer of the world and were forced instead to concentrate instead on Ms Middleton, who provided them with a constant source of fascination by walking down the street, drinking a cup of coffee or even – sensationally – walking while holding a cup of coffee at the same time.

Despite having more fame than the Beckhams, or even Jordan and Peter Andre, The Relationship was simply incapable of thriving in the heat of the public spotlight. With Ms Middleton clearly suffering from great nervous strain (as shown by her habit of referring to the lavatory as a 'toilet'), William's grandfather Prince Philip urged William to do the kindest thing. William, however, declined to dispatch Kate with a 12-bore or a white Fiat Panda and decided instead to put an end to The Relationship citing the pressures of his military career and a woman he met in a Bournemouth nightclub.

Prince William and Kate Middleton's Relationship was buried under acres of very dull newsprint. The officiant was a tedious man in a grey suit and the hymn was number 000, 'Oh God ~~Our Help In Ages Past~~, I'm Very Bored'.

Tom Cruise's Major Studio Deal
1992–2006

Tom Cruise's Major Studio Deal died suddenly this week after a long battle with declining box office returns. Despite The Deal's long illness, Mr Cruise forthrightly rejected all medical assistance for it, citing his deeply held religious beliefs and the difficulty of giving it an injection whilst he was bouncing up and down on its hospital bed.

Tom Cruise's Major Studio Deal came to prominence in 1992 when, desperate to shake off its image as the career of a diminutive, wooden-faced, pretty boy who expressed emotion and character chiefly by alternating between staring silently and shouting maniacally at his co-stars, it persuaded Tom Cruise to sign up with Paramount Studios in a contract that would guarantee him varied roles and vast sums of money.

In the ensuing years these varied roles were to come thick and fast. Who can forget *A Few Good Paychecks*, in which Tom played a diminutive, wooden-faced military lawyer – expressing emotion and character chiefly by alternating between staring silently and shouting maniacally at his co-stars: 'You want the money? You can't handle the money!' Next came *Jerry Morewages*, with Cruise wittily playing a diminutive, wooden-faced sports agent – expressing emotion and character chiefly by alternating between staring silently and shouting maniacally at his co-stars: 'Show me the money! So I can give it to the Scientologists! Did I mention I'm Operating Thetan Seven!?' Before long came the lead in top box office blockbuster *Mission: Unpayable*, with Cruise playing against type as a diminutive wooden-faced spy – expressing emotion and character chiefly by alternating between staring silently and shouting maniacally at his co-stars: 'I love her! This sofa will self-destruct in five seconds! Give me more money.'

In recent years, however, it became clear that the health of The Major Studio Deal was unwell. While Tom himself stuck to the task of promoting Scientology and acting weirdly on major chat shows, The Deal was often to be found desperately chasing after directors all over Hollywood in search of one more hit. Many saw its eventual decline as inevitable, especially those who sat through *War of the Worlds*.

Tom Cruise's Major Studio Deal passed away on Wednesday, leaving all its multi-million dollar fortune to a diminutive, wooden-faced actor, who expressed his deep emotion at the loss chiefly by alternating between staring silently and shouting maniacally at his fellow mourners. Friends of Mr Cruise say he will honour the memory of his Deal by continuing to surprise and delight audiences around the world with his ability to stretch himself. His next project is rumoured to be a biopic of Tom Thumb.

Civilisation

The Bonfire Night Guy
1606–5 November

The Bonfire Night Guy – that traditional, highly-flammable, stuffed effigy of Gunpowder Plotter Guido Fawkes – passed away on 5 November after succumbing to smoke inhalation and horrific third-degree burns. Fire brigades arriving at the scene of the fire were unable to save The Guy, as they were too busy eating baked potatoes and marshmallows cooked in the embers. Police called to the scene believe the fire may have been started deliberately and issued a statement saying: 'Ooh...! Look at the pretty colours...! Whooo...! I love fireworks me...!'

The Guy was born in 1606 when King James I declared 5 November an annual public holiday to celebrate his narrow escape from certain death in the previous year's Gunpowder Plot to blow up Parliament – while his loyal subjects commiserated a parliamentary failure almost as big as House of Commons Speaker Michael Martin.

Since a very early age, The Guy has been pushed around in carts and wheelbarrows prior to every Bonfire Night by gangs of children intent on taxing passers-by with the traditional cry of: 'A penny for the Guy, you wanker', not to mention, 'And we want your mobile phone and your trainers too'. After the goods have been fenced, any money remaining from the purchase of cheap booze and drugs is spent on arming themselves with potentially lethal fireworks with which to attack letter boxes, cars, buses, cyclists, cats, dogs, rabbits, hedgehogs, badgers, otters, horses, cows, donkeys, budgies, parrots, ospreys, hamsters, mice, rats and the elderly... before attacking other gangs of kids high on cheap booze and drugs and armed to the teeth with potentially lethal fireworks, the police, the fire brigade and the ambulance which has just arrived to treat their self-inflicted facial wounds and pick up their missing fingers.

The Guy was cremated in a private service attended by select friends and family in back gardens, public parks, village fetes and school playing fields across the country. At a special ceremony at Parliament, then Home Secretary John Reid commemorated the anniversary by holding The Guy without charge for 28 days before sending it by ceremonial rendition flight to an undisclosed site in Eastern Europe, where it was hanged, drawn and water-boarded by people in no way operating with the connivance of members of the CIA and the Bush administration.

The Guy is survived by The Burning Man, The Wicker Man, The Crazy World of Arthur Brown and Gordon Brown.

As a Dodo advisory: please don't forget to keep your cats, dogs and Catholics indoors on Bonfire Night.

Burying Bad News

*c.*100,000 BC–AD 2007

As a Dodo is sorry to relay the bad news that Burying Bad News itself has died following an unsuccessful attempt by the new Ministry of Justice to bury a massive increase in the cost of the ID card scheme on the day that the nation was paying its last respects to the glorious Premiership of Tony Blair.

Burying Bad News was born over 100,000 years ago, when news of Ug the Hunter's decision to dig his mastodon trap only one-foot deep – thus endangering the whole tribe – was released just after the neighbourhood volcano erupted, in a piece of news management so successful that it buried not only the bad news about the useless mastodon trap but also the entire village and everyone in it.

Burying Bad News quickly became a popular method for damage limitation and soon the practice came to the attention of politicians and personalities in the public eye. It was not long before anyone who was anyone was Burying Bad News: King Harold revealing his long-concealed 'large-piece-of-wood-in-the-eye allergy' on the day of William the Conqueror's victorious Hastings away match and Galileo confessing he had been using his newfangled telescope to spy on his neighbour's comely wife on the same day the newspapers were full of his claims about the Earth revolving around the Sun.

By the twentieth century Burying Bad News had truly

come of age. It was with the arrival of Tony Blair's New Labour government in 1997 that the dark arts of his spin doctors exalted Burying Bad News to the position of a new religion, as the British public were distracted from Peter Mandelson's manifold 'resignations' or the prime minister's failure to find weapons of mass destruction when they were announced on the day of either a major plot twist in *EastEnders* or news of a David Beckham haircut.

However, when an e-mail from Labour spin doctor Jo Moore suggesting that the attack on New York on 11 September might be a 'good day to bury bad news' was leaked, the age-old ruse began to weaken. The media became ever more cynical about news management and Burying Bad News found itself frequently blinking uncomfortably in the public spotlight.

So it was that, amid the gnashing and wailing/partying and champagne-cork-popping, as Mr Blair announced his plans to stand down as prime minister, the news of a further £840 million increase in the cost of digitally fingerprinting every man, woman, child, cat, dog and budgie in Britain (and charging them for it) was released. Sadly, the media were by now so jaded and mistrusting of government and so desperate for some real news to report that they pounced on the story like a herd of angry mastodons. And so it was that Burying Bad News passed away.

Burying Bad News will be buried on the day of a much more important story – like Tony Blair rising on the third day or Paris Hilton's release from prison. It is survived by bad news broadcasting, especially on BBC News 24 and Fox News.

Cleopatra's Beauty

*c.*51 BC–AD 2007

The reputation of Egypt's Queen Cleopatra VII for beauty – a reputation burnished down the ages by such great writers as Lucan, Shakespeare and the authors of short-lived sci-fi show *Cleopatra 2525* – has died, choked on a single Roman coin.

Born in about 51 BC, following Cleopatra's accession to the throne of Egypt at the age of 18, Cleopatra's reputation for beauty was rapidly spread about the whole of the known world, chiefly by drunken sailors for most of whom the last sight of a female was 'that dolphin off the coast of Asia Minor that was giving me the eye last week'. The fame of Cleopatra's Beauty grew even greater in 48 BC, when the Queen was usurped by her co-ruler and brother Ptolemy XIII and exiled.

By the time of Ptolemy's defeat by Julius Caesar later in 48 BC, Cleopatra's Beauty was known even in Rome. Keen to capitalise on the situation, the Queen decided to woo the Roman leader by having herself delivered to him in the palace at Alexandria rolled up inside a Persian carpet... which it now seems she probably didn't remove before wooing him. Caesar himself being a) a man, b) very important and c) a man – as well as being no great catch in the love stakes given that he was getting on a bit, frequently suffered fits and possessed a head of hair so sparse that even Donald Trump's barber would have been at a loss to deal with it – insisted that it be put about that he had been making love to the most beautiful woman in the world and thus a legend was born.

The Queen's allure gained even more lustre following Caesar's death, when she successfully wooed his closest follower, Mark Antony, with a combination of her charm, wit and – it would now seem – some very carefully arranged lighting. Their passionate relationship, in which they came close to ruling much of the known world, became renowned among the ancients, much as the relationship of David and Victoria Beckham is today. Its romantic demise, with each killing themselves at the thought of the other's loss, inspired generations. Centuries later William Shakespeare recorded the Queen's extraordinary loveliness in his *Anthony and Cleopatra*, although his judgment in this regard may well be brought into question by the fact he did insist she be played by a young boy. Soon she was being played by the greatest beauties of every age from Elizabeth Taylor to... er... Judi Dench.

Having survived more than 2,000 years, Cleopatra's Beauty breathed its last on Valentine's Day 2007, when the unearthing of a coin bearing the heads of both Anthony and Cleopatra by Newcastle University revealed that the two of them were so ugly that, if they did spend long nights of passion together, each probably insisted the other wear a bag over their head throughout.

Cleopatra's Beauty will be buried at the Nicky-Hambleton Jones Church of the Botox-Frozen Forehead. It is survived by Cleo Lane, Cleo Rocos, the Renault Clio and a production of *Anthony and Cleopatra* starring Anne Widdecombe as the Queen of Egypt.

Democracy

*c.*508 BC–AD 2007

It is hard to exaggerate the sadness that will be felt (outside political circles) at the death, confirmed today by a group of senior psephologists, of Democracy in Britain and America.

Democracy, or 'force of the people', was born around 508 BC in the ancient Greek city state of Athens, where it granted power to all the people – except unreliable types like slaves, women, children or foreigners – to govern themselves. The Athenians established several important democratic traditions, including the practice of ballots, the separation of the legislature, executive and the courts and, during the Peloponnesian War, the tendency to try and suspend the whole idea of Democracy at the first sign of trouble.

Assailed on all sides by those who felt that letting the people govern themselves was about as wise as leaving your wife alone with Zeus for more than a picosecond, Democracy was to become distinctly unfashionable due to its tendency to fall to whoever could pay their soldiers the most. Throughout the Ancient world it was replaced by the rule of Emperors, who at least tended to dress in chic purple outfits and have the kind of social lives that could keep a whole empire's worth of people gossiping for centuries. Unfortunately, they too fell out of fashion. In Europe they were largely replaced by Kings, who were quite like Emperors apart from having much worse table manners, a tendency to go round in armour all the time and a preference for beheading and burning at the stake as opposed to crucifixion and throwing to the lions.

Despite such attitudes, Democracy was content to bide its time, sure in the knowledge that the tide of fashion would turn once more in its favour. Gradually it crept back into the public gaze in such places as the Polish-Lithuanian Commonwealth and Iceland's *Althing*. In England it gave rise to the creation of Parliament, for which all people were allowed to vote, except unreliable types like women, children, foreigners, the landless, the poor or anyone the King wasn't keen on. Soon democratic institutions were emerging elsewhere, reaching their finest flowering in the institutions set up under the Constitution of the United States of America, whose aim of preventing the good people of the US from being ruled over by dubiously-installed, hereditary leaders named George was achieved for the next 200 years.

It was at the turn of the twentieth century that Democracy began to show signs of ill health. The first of these was the fact that, despite its frequently proclaimed popularity, many countries continued to show no interest in it whatsoever, even when that interest was invited at gunpoint. The second was the realisation that, thanks to a combination of first-past-the-post elections, the ever-greater sophistication of pollsters and political machines and ever-greater emphasis on attracting so-called 'swing voters', politicians had increasingly concentrated on ever smaller parts of the electorate. Indeed, by the early twenty-first century, throughout Britain and

America Democracy found itself dependent on just two voters. In Great Britain the one person upon whom it depended was a man called Dave who had 1.2 kids, had recently upgraded his Vauxhall Vectra to a BMW 3 series and bought the *Daily Mail* each day – despite being scared witless by Melanie Phillips's columns – because his wife liked the human interest pieces and faddy diet tips; in America, it was a guy called Bud from the Mid-West who drove an SUV, believed the best way to stop people killing each other was to buy more semi-automatic weapons and who watched anything with Ann Coulter on because his wife thought she talked a lot of sense and he had a bit of a thing for dominant blondes. Having realised the enormous power Dave and Bud wielded, the pair were instantly crowned rulers of the Anglo-Saxon world, after which they dropped bombs on Canada, Australia and New Zealand just to prove they meant business.

Democracy will be buried at the Church of St Tony the Straight Kinda Guy. Bud and Dave have requested that no flowers be delivered, only oil (Bud) and Marmite (Dave). Democracy is survived by US Plutocracy, Russian Oligarchy, British Cronyism, Chinese Corporatism, Iranian Theocracy, Iraqi Anarchy and assorted Despotisms, Tyrannies and Kleptocracies.

Freedom

*c.*100,000 BC–AD 2006

A fun-loving child of the swinging 100,000 BCs, Freedom was always known for her liberating, devil-may-care attitude and easy-going views on everything from drugs to sexual morality. Often caricatured as a hippie, beneath her happy-go-lucky persona lay a resolute fighter for liberty and a believer in the inalienable rights of each and every being. From her time hanging around with the notorious hairy hominid *Homo sapiens* to today, Freedom campaigned for the downtrodden, beginning in her youth with her fight for the right to pick fleas off one's mate (a right still enjoyed today by many Glastonbury Festival-goers).

By the second millennium BC, Freedom was encouraging the Israelites to say goodbye to 'the Man' ('the Man' being 'Pharaoh') and 'find themselves' on a walkabout amid the deserts of the Middle East. Only two millennia later she was persuading young Goths and Vandals from all over Europe to come to Rome to hold a sit-in and 'express themselves'... which they did with great gusto, pretty much all over the place.

In the centuries that followed, Freedom wandered the globe, 'fighting the power' wherever it could be found. By the late eighteenth century she was dancing the night away with the likes of Thomas Paine and the heroes of the American War of Independence. During this time she also fell in with a group of French exchange students, going off to Paris to hold a mind-blowing (or, more precisely, head chopping) revolution. Not long after she was wigging out with newly-freed slaves before going on to explore her womanhood with the suffragettes, then donning a pink cowboy hat and chaps (and very little else) to march for gay rights.

Such a controversial lifestyle could not help but to attract enemies. Over the years Freedom was assailed by powers temporal and spiritual... all of whom wanted to have as much Freedom as possible for themselves (often including the freedom to amass vast luxury, to oppress anyone they didn't like and, strangely enough, to sleep with any member of the animal kingdom they chose) while denying it to everybody else. Despite their attacks, Freedom carried on untroubled.

While Freedom managed to come through her wild life unscathed, many of her oldest friends began to show signs of paranoia, perhaps due to the bitter experiences of centuries fighting oppression, perhaps due to excessive alcohol intake and cocaine abuse in their youth. Several developed an obsession with ensuring Freedom's safety. Fearful that she might be attacked by 'evildoers', and despite the protests of Freedom herself, they insisted she leave her home less and less and then only with an armed escort. Eventually, those who claimed to be her closest companions confined her to her room, where they kept her under constant surveillance by CCTV. Deprived of the liberty she always craved, Freedom withered away.

Freedom is survived by her complete biometric data, surveillance files and CCTV footage, which will remain on a centralised database for all eternity.

Free Will

*c.*450 BC–AD 2007

As a Dodo has no choice but to report the passing of Free Will, which – after many years of illness – has been declared dead by a team of neuroscientists from Germany, London and Oxford.

Free Will was born in the philosophical schools of ancient Greece in about 450 BC when, following Socrates's conclusion that 'the good – being identical with the true – imposes itself irresistibly on the will as on the intellect when distinctly apprehended and that every man necessarily wills his greatest good, and his actions are merely means to this end', one of his students punched him in the face for being a dreadful old bore.

Free Will was an unpopular child – frequently getting into fights with philosophers who felt their decision to gang up on Free Will and attempt to beat it to a pulp were all preordained by bearded men on Mount Olympus given to chucking thunderbolts about and changing into swans and bulls to ravish young maidens. Later on it would grow up to be an unpopular adult, frequently getting into fights with logical, biological and theological determinists who thought their decision to gang up on Free Will was preordained by past events, the contents of their genes or a bearded man in the sky with a strange resemblance to Dr Rowan Williams.

AS A DODO

After two millennia of hard knocks, and a succession of increasingly repressive British home secretaries, Free Will first began to complain of feeling unwell when millions of Britons felt compelled to vote New Labour into power in 1997, while in 2000 millions of Americans thought they were voting the Democrats into power but were told otherwise by Jeb Bush and Fox News. Free Will continued about its business but its health was repeatedly called into question after receiving a rapid series of heavy blows in the form of speed cameras, CCTV, biometric passports, DNA testing, ASBOs, 28-day detention without trial and the continuing success of the musicals of Andrew Lloyd Webber.

The final blow for Free Will came when it was revealed that neuroscientists from the Max Planck Institute for Human Cognitive and Brain Sciences in Germany, with colleagues from University College London and Oxford University, had developed a new technique that allows them to look deep inside a person's brain and predict their intentions before they act. On making the discovery they immediately informed Free Will, which promptly did as it was told and died.

Free Will has asked to be cremated in a secular service but will instead be held for 28 days before being buried at St John the Reid's Church of Thoughtcrime. It is survived by the National Lottery.

Limbo

0–2006

Unbaptised souls throughout the crystal spheres are today mourning the loss of their former home, Limbo. The news comes following the decision of Pope Benedict to abolish Limbo due to a) the fact that the concept of unbaptised children being forever tainted by original sin is inconsistent with a modern interpretation of the gospels and b) the feelings of bitterness he has held towards the very word 'limbo' ever since that time he tried to shimmy under a low, low pole in his mitre while on a Sandals holiday in Jamaica.

Limbo was a bleak and lonely place on the borders of reality, free from the torments of hell such as eternal fires, burning sand and double-glazing salesmen but forever excluded from the delights of heaven, such as being surrounded by devout theists for all eternity. Despite this it proved unpopular with visitors, the only tourists to that place of grim non-existence in the last 2,000 years being Jesus, Dante and anyone who has ever sat down in front of *Countdown* for more than three minutes.

Despite its unprepossessing aspect, for much of its 2,000-year existence Limbo was home to some of the greatest minds to have existed before the birth of Christ including Homer and Virgil but sadly not Marge, Bart and Lisa, or any of Virgil's fellow *Thunderbirds*. While the unbaptised are said to be distraught at saying goodbye to the only home some of them have known for the past two millennia, other residents of Limbo took the news of its death philosophically – the residents in question being Plato, Aristotle, Zeno and Socrates. Zeno in particular was untroubled by the news having proved beyond all possible doubt that Limbo could never be destroyed, just as an arrow could never, philosophically speaking, reach its target... exactly two minutes before Pope Benedict decided to wipe it out of existence.

Limbo is survived by Purgatory, Hell and watching Adam Sandler movies.

Problems

*c.*100,000 BC–AD 2007

An international panel of scientists has concluded that the last Problem in Great Britain is dead, out-competed by its distant transatlantic cousin, the Challenge.

The first Problem arose in about 100,000 BC – at roughly the time *Homo sapiens* developed the capacity for rational thought – when caveman Ug realised facing a stampeding mammoth with a bit of tree branch with a flint strapped to the end might not be such a great idea. Over the millennia many Problems were to present themselves to Ug and his successors, including hunger, illness, and the fact the neighbouring tribe had developed sharper pieces of flint to tie to their tree branches. As the years passed and worries about neighbouring tribes having superior bits of flint turned to ones about neighbouring city-states having pointier bronze swords, so humanity discovered whole new Problems to worry about, including how to work out the area of a circle, whether the Earth revolved around the Sun or vice versa and how to govern a bunch of people armed with incredibly pointy bronze swords.

With each Problem, mankind was driven to discover a new solution. Soon it had discovered things like gravity, medicine, hot and cold running water and nuclear weapons, and was entitled to sit back and feel very happy with itself, although a bit nervous about all those nuclear weapons.

It was in the 1960s that Problems met their rival, as Wall Street marketing men realised that people found Problems awkward and negative and the business of having to find solutions to them rather tiresome. Searching for an alternative they stumbled upon the Challenge, a term redolent of acts of derring-do like climbing Mount Everest and, like climbing Mount Everest, having an air of being something one didn't have to worry about at all if one didn't want to.

Soon Challenges were pushing Problems out of their natural territory. Anywhere people wanted to sugar unpalatable truths or gloss over their own deficiencies, there Challenges could be found. Among those swiftest to cast Problems out of their language were politicians. Pupils with learning Problems were liberated from the shackles of ignorance by being redesignated 'learning challenged', people with mobility Problems found themselves leaping from their wheelchairs and Zimmer frames, eager to welcome the newly-coined Challenges that injury or Mother Nature had strewn in their, somewhat erratic and very short, paths.

By the noughties Problems had almost died out in public discourse, so much so that in late 2007, politicians across the globe declared that they had dealt with all their Problems by converting them to Challenges. Within days the nations of the world were following suit.

Problems, having been conclusively identified as living-challenged, will be buried at the Church of St Judas the Slightly Iffy on Saturday. They are survived by Challenges, Small Presentational Issues and Downright Lies.

Royal Mail's Universal Service
1840–2007

The Last Post has been sounded for Royal Mail's Universal Service following the news that Royal Mail was losing 6p on each stamped letter it delivered – and losing most of the cheques, credit cards and birthday money contained in those letters themselves.

Royal Mail was founded in 1516, the misbegotten offspring of Henry VIII, who established a Master of the Posts to ensure that his billets-doux were delivered to the correct girlfriend – sparing him both embarrassment and unnecessary expenditure on royal executioners.

Royal Mail led a privileged and sheltered life – delivering romantic quatrains to mistresses, declarations of war to cousins who ruled enemy powers and notifications of having won a free entry in *Ye Olde Readers' Digeste* draw to courtiers – until 1653 when it was forced to go public by Charles I. Sadly the King's plans were stalled for several years after his plan to close Parliament was incorrectly delivered to a Mr O. Cromwell. Over the following decades Royal Mail continued its work as usual, letting neither snow, nor rain, nor Black Death stay its couriers from the slow completion of those rounds they could be bothered to deal with before bunging any excess post in the nearest open sewer.

Change came in 1840, when Royal Mail gave birth to The Universal Service with its uniform penny post – allowing urchins, mill-owners and philanthropists alike to send mail to whomsoever they liked as well as introducing the dreaded hobby, philately.

Despite this The Universal Service became a popular way of delivering letters, parcels and bombs across the nation, until the effects of the global market began to take their toll. In 2000, battered by constant criticism of its high cost and tardy and erroneous deliveries, Royal Mail first tried to escape its poor image by disguising itself under the name Consignia. Within days it was discovered, after thousands of its new brochures bound for potential customers were found dumped in a wheelie-bin behind the sorting office. Forced to confront the ugly truth it reverted to its original name and spent its final years harried from pillar box to post office by constant jibes about thieving posties and over-priced stamps. In a desperate bid to stop the rot Royal Mail began to close rural post offices and calculate postage on increasingly eccentric scales – weight, size, colour of envelope, popularity of recipient and ferocity of their dog – but to no avail. It was finally licked this week.

The body of Royal Mail's Universal Service will be parcelled up and posted to the Great Sorting Office in the Sky, but will be delivered to a Mr G. S. Orting of Skye and will remain unopened for a number of weeks before being returned to sender... and delivered to Roy & Alma, The Ale House, Cirencester. It is survived by thousands of private courier companies who guarantee next day delivery and modern modes of communication such as e-mail, texting and shouting very loudly.

A Simple Cup of Coffee

*c.*Ninth Century–2007

A Simple Cup of Coffee has been drained from its cup for the last time after being swamped by the planet's unchecked demand for increasingly baroque and bastardised frappaccinos, mochaccinnos and latteccinos served by overworked immigrants living in fear of being docked pay for failing to say 'Have a nice day' with the company-approved sincere expression.

A Simple Cup of Coffee was first brewed in Ethiopia in the ninth century, proving so stimulating that, after drinking just one cup, coffee exporters stayed up for six straight months, only falling asleep after flogging gallons of the new beverage as far as Egypt and Yemen.

By the seventeenth century the new brew had reached Europe, with the Dutch in particular enjoying the benefits of increased blood pressure and heart rate of A Simple Cup of Coffee in their world-famous coffee houses, so much so that they were soon forced to start taking massive tokes on the nearest available spliff to calm themselves down.

Soon London merchants were gathering to discuss shipping news in Lloyd's Coffee House, where their massive intake led them to become so excited that they set up a whole stock market, whose vast profits were able to fund the expansion of the British Empire as well as allowing the traders to afford ever greater quantities of their favourite stimulants, thus encouraging major South American exports... and several coffee growers as well.

The practice of stumbling from one's bed towards the stove to brew up an energising cup was to spread to the New World – but not until the third cup of coffee had hit the spot. Indeed, the American War of Independence was started by the craze for a good cup of mud after jittery Bostonians rejected a shipment of tea, angrily throwing it into the harbour – even though the water wasn't boiling *and* they hadn't added the milk first.

Soon the world was enslaved by this narcotic drink, with only a few plucky Britons holding out against its tyranny. But as the British Empire crumbled, even this bastion of tea-drinking limeys began to succumb. Americans, however, were growing bored with A Simple Cup of Coffee and had begun experimenting with new ways of ingesting their favourite drug: mixing it with cold sugary colas, adding it to the water supply, cross-breeding it with flavoured syrups and giving it faux Italian names with the suffix '-ccino'.

The fatal blow came with the introduction of Shower Shock soap, which released the same amount of caffeine into the bloodstream as a couple of cups of coffee as users lathered themselves in the shower to achieve that roasted fresh, smell in the mornings. Appalled at the news, A Simple Cup of Coffee expired in a wave of bitter suds.

A Simple Cup of Coffee was buried at St Arbucks Church of the Decaf Super Grande Skinny Mochalattefrappaespressoccino. The service was conducted by Gunther from *Friends*. It is survived by A Decaf Super Grande Skinny Mochalattefrappaespressoccino... and A Nice Cup of Tea.

Smoking in Public

c.Sixteenth Century–2007

Smokers are shouting short-temperedly at their partners and downing their pints with extra haste in memory of Smoking in Public, which has gasped its last, wheezy breath and gone to the Great Ashtray in the Sky.

Smoking in Public took its first puffs after Sir Walter Raleigh finally gave up his attempt to convince Elizabethans to adopt the practice of smoking potatoes and putting lashings of salt and vinegar on their deep-fried tobacco, and instead filled his pipe with some rough shag he'd brought back from the New World.

Thanks to its addictive qualities (and the fact that it makes you look dead sexy... usually about thirty years before it makes you look dead) Smoking in Public became hugely popular. It was not without its critics, however: in *A Counterblaste to Tobacco*, 1604, King James I himself warned that smoking was 'A custom loathsome to the eye, hateful to the nose, harmful to the brain, dangerous to the lungs, and in the blacke stinking fume thereof, neerest resembling the horrible Stigian smoke of the pit that is bottomelesse', much to the amazement of courtiers who were unaware he had ever been to Birmingham.

Despite knowledge of the harmful effects of inhaling tobacco smoke, seventeenth-century man, woman, child and, in some circuses, chimpanzee took up the habit with gusto – puffing away without a care in the world – assuming that the blood they were coughing up was just the harmless first sign of tuberculosis or plague.

Smoking in Public caught on like wildfire, as – during hot, dry summers – did much of the surrounding countryside. By the twentieth century, stoked by popular images of Hollywood stars moodily inhaling a Lucky Strike whilst eyeing up the femme fatale, examining the dead body or relaxing after the train had entered the tunnel, everyone – from new born babes to grandfathers (quite literally) breathing their last – was sucking on a fag, pipe or hookah.

In the post-war years, however, people began to realise they *were* alone with a Strand and that the 'busy day at the crematorium' smell that hung about them might be the cause. With the arrival of evidence that nicotine was more addictive than *Deal or No Deal* (but not quite as harmful), Smoking in Public came under pressure to pack it in, knock it on the head, go cold turkey and try patches, hypnotism or that silly ceramic pipe that everyone's too embarrassed to use.

Even the appearance of suaveness, brilliance and emotional intensity derived from inhaling filterless Gauloises began to pall. With increased awareness of the fatal consequences of smoking – that unique kipper-factory odour, Judith Chalmers-style leathery skin and a voice deeper than Mariella Frostrup's – Smoking in Public began to cough, hack, wheeze and expectorate colourfully. Complaining of breathlessness, Smoking in Public exhaled a final plume of blue-grey smoke and was extinguished.

Smoking in Public was cremated in a private ceremony. The congregation sang hymn 486 'Smoke Gets in Your Eyes… and Your Throat, Lungs, Heart, and May Harm Your Unborn Baby'.

Terrorism
1793–2007

Terrorism was born in 1793 in France, the younger brother of the famously attractive triplets Liberté, Egalité and Fraternité, who were the toast of the land during the ongoing French Revolution. Though it was later to set out on its own, Terrorism's early years were spent in close proximity to the state, ousting its elder sisters from the national bosom in the hope that false arrests, conviction on the flimsiest of evidence and a surveillance society could be nurtured in their place. Arm in arm with Citizen Robespierre and Madame Guillotine it wandered up and down France, stirring fear in the hearts of all it met and a desire to hide among all it didn't (a role today played by itinerant Mormons, Jehovah's Witnesses and chuggers).

Like many a youngster, Terrorism began to tire of hanging around with the parents and decided to strike out on its own. Soon it was hanging around with anarchists and plotting to bring down the state, or suggesting to the inhabitants of colonial outposts that it might be a good means of ridding themselves of their imperial oppressors (or in the case of T. E. Lawrence, a really good excuse for mucking around on camels in a keffiyeh), before going on to hang out with just about anyone with a grievance, a liking for blowing things up and easy access to large quantities of fertiliser.

From the latter part of the twentieth century, Terrorism came to be a significant force in global politics, instilling widespread fear, taking thousands of lives and inflicting numerous episodes of *24* upon the world. Where once people merely had the prospect of nuclear annihilation to keep them awake at night, now they had the possibility of being shot, gassed, tortured or blown up (either by the terrorists or by Jack Bauer) as they went about their daily business to keep them from the arms of Morpheus. Yet not even this was enough for Terrorism, whose attention-seeking and destructive behaviour had merely been an attempt to return to the bosom of the state, where it could go back to practices such as imprisoning the citizenry without trial, indulging in constant surveillance of the public at large and abrogating the liberty of the people.

Happily, we are assured by John Reid, the father of The Office for Security and Counter-Terrorism, that his new offspring's 'faster, brighter and more agile response' to Terrorism gives us the brightest prospect of putting an end to this dreadful scourge... and if that fails it can simply put Terrorism out of business by doing much of its work for it.

Terrorism will be buried in an undisclosed location by men in balaclavas. It is survived by freedom fighters, jihadis, fedayeen, guerillas and assorted other nutters in quasi-military dress who think the best way of resolving a dispute is to bomb the hell out of something (as opposed to those of the same opinion without balaclavas, who are often in government).

The Twenty-first Century
2001–2006

The population of the Vatican was today mourning The Twenty-first Century, after it was declared dead by Pope Benedict XVI in a brief address from St Peter's Square.

It appears from His Holiness's speech that, despite being born in a vigorous bout of distrust of modernity brought on by an early infection with the millennium bug, the still young century had been showing increasing signs of ill health over the past six years. In particular there was evidence that it had inherited several afflictions from its parents, The Nineteenth and Twentieth Centuries, including freedom of thought, belief in Darwinian evolution, women's liberation, the unfortunate practice of prosecuting priests who wish to display their affections to young choir boys and a distressing lack of crusades in the Holy Land. The Century having failed to improve despite the finest leech-craft of the Vatican's doctors, the Holy Father eventually found himself with no alternative but to administer the last rites to The Century... whilst also administering a red hot poker to The Century's fundament.

Speaking to an assembled crowd of serfs, freemen, pardoners, clerkes, reeves, apothecaries and villeins, Pope

Benedict announced that henceforth The Twenty-first Century will be replaced by the ever-reliable Fourteenth Century, adding that from now on the Sun will travel around the Earth, the Black Death will be endemic across Europe and the best way of improving Christian–Muslim relations will be at the end of a long and pointy lance. His Holiness's address was greeted by rapturous applause from the crowd, though the effect was somewhat lessened when several of the lepers' arms fell off. Fortunately the festive air was soon restored by the burning of an assortment of witches.

The Twenty-first Century was buried on Saturday morning in a moving ceremony, marred only when Pope Benedict told the assembled relatives that The Twenty-first Century was 'evil and inhuman', although officials later explained His Holiness had not meant to cause any offence.

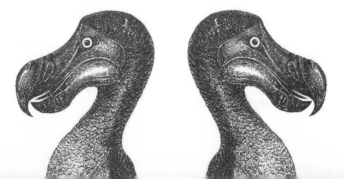

Culture and Entertainment

Albert Camus's *The Outsider*

1942–2006

Albert Camus's *The Outsider* (*L'Etranger*) died today. Or maybe yesterday. The world-famous absurdist novel, about a man who shoots an Arab for no reason and then refuses to show remorse for what he has done, was wounded in a fatal explosion of irony at the weekend when it was revealed that the book was at the heart of President George Bush's summer reading.

The Outsider was born in 1942 to a union of absurdist philosophy and the retired goalkeeper of the University of Algiers second XI. A precocious child, by the late 1940s it was already to be seen hanging around with the likes of Jack Kerouac, its habit of wearing black polo-neck sweaters and chain-smoking Gauloises cigarettes, along with its habitual cry of '*Je suis l'étranger*, daddio' making it easy to spot on its trips outside the smoke-filled interiors of bebop jazz clubs.

Tiring of its dim surroundings, *The Outsider* soon found itself migrating to university campuses across the globe. It came to Britain in the 1950s where it soon became famed among duffel-coated male students as the key to French philosophy, to the coolness of alienation and to copping off with female students. With its influence ever-increasing, by the late 1960s *The Outsider* was to be found at the head of protests and sit-ins across the globe, from the riot-torn streets of

Paris to the slightly disordered desks of the Pinner College upper sixth form geography class.

As both it and its friends drifted into middle age, *The Outsider* began to abandon its radical past, eventually being persuaded to appear on A-level syllabuses, where it was to confuse generations of teenagers. Despite this it was occasionally to be found, looking a little tattered, hanging around in coffee bars with would-be intellectuals, a cigarette dangling from its lips, still trying to impress young women.

Albert Camus's *The Outsider* will be buried in a student flat, beneath several posters of Che Guevara, some Leonard Cohen CDs and a rucksack full of dirty washing due to be taken back to mum next weekend. Anyone who does not cry will be hanged.

Blackpool's Las Vegas Dreams
2006–2007

The people of Blackpool are today jumping up and down on their 'Kiss Me Quick' hats and snapping their little sticks of Blackpool rock in two as they remember their dreams of building a new Las Vegas on the shores of the Irish Sea, dreams which were brought to an untimely end on Tuesday with the decision to award the government's new 'super-casino' to Manchester.

Blackpool's Las Vegas Dreams were born in May 2006, the offspring of a government desperate to grab itself a nice slice of the gambling profit pie and a council desperate to regenerate a seaside town haunted by an unholy mixture of the vomiting remnants of the last few stag and hen parties unable to afford the low-cost airfare to Dublin or Prague and bewildered gangs of nostalgic pensioners wandering the streets in the mistaken belief that the thriving resort of their youth hadn't turned into a place with all the charm of a Glaswegian proctologist.

Soon Blackpool was dreaming of transforming itself into a new Las Vegas – its badly-suited doormen and surly one-armed bandit attendants transformed into uniformed bellhops and unctuous one-armed bandit attendants, its low-grade lap-dancing clubs transformed into high-class lap-dancing clubs and its 'world-famous' tower, illuminations and pleasure beach transformed into attractions that might stand a chance of being famous outside the north of England, not to mention around the world. Up and down the sea front, attraction owners fell into reveries as they contemplated the possibility of swapping the daily grind of separating bored teens, problem gamblers and lonely pensioners from their pennies for the pleasant task of separating bored rich people, problem gamblers and lonely pensioners from their life-savings.

Blackpool's Las Vegas Dreams were not to be fulfilled. Their death was announced by The Casino Advisory Panel, who decided on Tuesday to award the rights to build the new super-casino in Manchester rather than the seaside resort, presumably on the basis that the north-west's leading city was the only location with a high enough murder rate to justify Grissom and the gang jetting over from the original Las Vegas to launch yet another extension to the *CSI* franchise.

Blackpool's Las Vegas Dreams will be buried under the floor of the Tower Ballroom on Friday. They are survived by an ever-declining number of tourists and a massive increase in problem gambling in Manchester.

The Da Vinci Code Litigation
2006–2007

In presenting this obituary for The Da Vinci Code *Litigation, which recently passed away, we at* As a Dodo *wish to apologise for our reporter on the scene, who it would appear was so affected by what he saw that he has absorbed more than a little of* The Da Vinci Code *style. Please forgive us.*

Renowned conspiracy theorists 59-year-old Michael Baigent and 64-year-old Richard Leigh staggered through the neo-gothic archway of the Victorian Royal Courts of Justice yesterday. They lunged for the nearest reporter they could see, a representative of *As a Dodo*. Grabbing my Gannex mac forcefully they told me a grim tale of dark conspiracy, of the death of their beloved *The Da Vinci Code* Litigation at the hands of a secret society and of vast amounts of publicity for *The Holy Blood and The Holy Grail*. In the crisp air of a March afternoon in London they told me The Truth.

Now at last I can reveal The Truth about *The Da Vinci Code* Litigation to the global world.

It is time.

The Da Vinci Code Litigation was born in 2006. It was the child of two men, Michael Baigent and Richard Leigh, and of the billions of dollars made by dashing, cardigan-wearing author Dan Brown. Together Baigent and Leigh had built up one of the greatest conspiracy theories ever known, a theory that could make them millions. All they had to do was claim Jesus Christ had married Mary Magdalene and had children, that their descendants married into the ancient line of ancient French Kings, the Merovingians, and that a secret society planned one day to restore them to the French throne of France. They knew they could do it. They wouldn't even need any evidence. People are stupid.

The plan was brilliant. The pair published a book, *The Holy Blood and the Holy Grail*. People believed it. But now the plan was under threat. The threat came from the sinister figure of sinister Dan Brown who, beneath his dark jacket, dark turtleneck sweater and light chinos, was a secret member of the Society of Authors. Brown saw the genius of *The Holy Blood and the Holy Grail*. He knew he had to act. He spent hours in dark corners of the hallowed halls of his local Barnes and Noble bookstore, reading through the book. With a trembling hand he noted down the book's ideas in his leather-bound notebook. Now they were his.

Leigh and Baigent blanched white when they saw the product of Brown's work: *The Da Vinci Code*. They ripped it furiously from the shelves, flipping rapidly through its pages with white-knuckled hands. In it they saw all their ideas. They even saw themselves, cunningly disguised in a codex of extreme cunningness, as Sir Leigh Teabing. Their plan had been exposed to the world. And now it was making millions.

Swiftly, Leigh and Baigent set out quickly for revenge. They ran speedily to the murky halls of the Royal Courts of Justice. They were met by three men, their thinning hair covered by horsehair wigs, their aged bodies covered by blood red robes. One of the men stepped forward.

'Mr Leigh, Mr Baigent,' he said, chillingly close, 'You have no case – these crazy ideas of yours are far too general to provide the basis for litigation.'

Leigh and Baigent turned to each other. How could these men have known? There was only one answer: these 'judges' must have been members of the Society of Authors too. As they looked behind the men in front of them, towards the part of the Royal Courts of Justice that was named the Bear Garden by Queen Victoria in 1882, Leigh and Baigent saw before them the sight they dreaded. On the floor lay their precious Litigation, strangled to death. They fled.

The quest for *The Da Vinci Code* Litigation is the quest to kneel before the bones of Leigh and Baigent's hopes of millions, to kneel before the hopes of the outcast ones and weep. Now it is over, ended in the ancient Royal Courts of Justice on a floor on which Romans might once have trod if it had been built before 1882.

The As a Dodo *editors add:* The Da Vinci Code *Litigation will be buried under massive legal bills. It is survived by ludicrous conspiracy theories, the works of Dan Brown and millions of people who wouldn't know a decent book if it bit them on the arse.*

The Eurovision Song Contest
1956–2007

The Eurovision Song Contest has met its Waterloo, warbling its last 'boom-bang-a-le-boop-boop' and fielding its final trans-gendered contestant dolled up in the kind of spangly costume not seen since *Space: 1999*, after tactical voting saw Serbia snatch victory from more deserving musical talent... and Britain's Scooch.

The Eurovision Song Contest was born in the post-war years to foster European co-operation and unite a continent torn asunder by world war and the lack of an incredibly cheesy music contest for Terry Wogan to laugh at.

It was in 1956 that Eurovision first chose to abandon the continent's vast musical heritage and take up the mittel-European oompah-oompah beat and the nonsensically onomatopoeic lyric in a seven-nation tussle in Switzerland – a contest won by the Swiss, thanks in part to strong support from a grateful German nation which couldn't remember where it had left all that gold.

In its early years, winners of The Eurovision Song Contest were guaranteed to go on to even greater success as mature, ground-breaking songwriters and performers – or at least that's what the organisers claimed. Despite this, the cream of popular musicians from across the continent fought tooth and nail not to take part: The Beatles turning down the opportunity to represent their country with 'All You Need Is Boom-Bang-A-Le-Boop-Boop Ob-La-Di, Love', Jacques Brel failing to favour Europe with his up-tempo 'La Vie Est Mort Doobie-Doo', and Nana Mouskouri only agreeing to enter if she could avoid disgracing her homeland by pretending to be from Luxembourg.

The sweet music of a harmonious musical competition was soon drowned out. Harmony and melody gave way to simple Euro-disco rhythms, grating vocals and inane choruses lifted from Esperanto greetings cards. Baltic states and former Soviet satellites shared out their votes in a collective fashion, Greece and Cyprus supported each other through thick and thin and everyone voted for Ireland time and time again in order to avoid the crippling financial burden of hosting the contest.

It was in Helsinki, however, that the once-great competition was finally reduced to a mockery. Throughout the evening, plucky western European band after plucky western European band was felled in its prime by the massed texted votes of the Eastern Voting Bloc. Even Scooch, Britain's plucky band of ~~crap~~ crack musicians, cunningly disguised as cabin stewards on Air Latex, received *nul points* after *nul points*, leaving Serbia to snatch the laurel crown. Thus was the death knell sounded (in the wrong key) and so Eurovision was no more.

The Eurovision Song Contest will be buried at the European Broadcasting Union Church of St Jude the Pointless. The service will be conducted by two perma-tanned celebrities you've never heard of, with a mocking audio commentary on their performance provided by the Reverend Wogan. The congregation will sing Hymn number 278 'Oobie-Shalala-Bim-Bam-Bom-De-Doo-Doo-Doo-De-Dah-Dah-Dah-Wopbopaloobop-Doobie-Tra-la-la', accompanied by Mr Harris on the Church Souzaphone.

Intelligent Science Programmes on British Television

1936–2006

The As a Dodo *team apologise for the following obituary. We were unaware at the time of commissioning that the staff member assigned to the task had, in fact, worked for BBC television's* Horizon *programme. It is hoped that, given the importance of the obituary, our readers will forgive the style in which it has been drafted. We have left the author's notes in the text, on the grounds that they supply full explanation for his* ~~execution~~ *dismissal.*

Scientists in Britain have made a discovery that will transform life across the planet. More than seventy years after they first appeared, Intelligent Science Programmes are facing extinction. By the end of 2006 scientists predict that they will all be dead, wiped out by a cataclysm that we have done nothing to prevent... and the world as we know it will come to an end.

Intelligent Science Programmes first appeared in about 1936, when the mighty Tyrannosaurus Reith dominated the television world. His dreadful mission to 'inform, educate and entertain' forced the tiny Intelligent Science Programmes to find an ecological niche [term a bit complex for our audience?] where they had to make difficult things understandable to people without patronising them.

Thanks to the 'selective pressure of their environment' [got this from a text book, should we just say intelligent design?], Intelligent Science Programmes soon spread throughout the televisual ecosphere [not sure this means anything but it sounds good] to any place where a spark of brightness could be found. Vast Intelligent Science Programming beasts soon arose, with giants such as Dr Jacob Bronowski's *Ascent of Man* and David Attenborough's *Life on Earth* battling for the attention of the public and *The Royal Institution Christmas Lectures* threatening to devour their children. But already The Programmes' existence was facing a challenge, a challenge that would see them wiped out... and the fate of the world in the balance.

By the mid 1980s a new breed was beginning to dominate the tellysphere [there, that's even better]. With the fundamental rules of commissioning science destroyed by light regulation, increasing TV channels and people with media studies degrees, [hey – that's me!] soon Intelligent Science Programmes were facing competition from new stupid science programmes, such as *The Boy Whose Anus Ate His Brain*, *Why Cookery is Dead Clever* and *Da Vinci's Bible Alien Code: The Truth*. Scientists across Britain were worried... could it mean the end of the world?

By the early noughties Intelligent Science Programmes were dying. Many were wiped out completely, while others found themselves evolving [could put off the creationists?] into new forms. By 2006, confirmation that the last Intelligent Science Programme had dumbed down came with the news that the latest edition of *Horizon* would feature a comedian and TV personality talking to chimpanzees.

Intelligent Science Programmes were buried in a late night slot on some obscure channel where they will never be seen again.

[Was this OK? I reckon it might be too clever for the punters. I'll dumb down the second draft and add in something about Britney Spears.]

The Long Good Friday
1980–2007

Lovers of British films are today gathering to scatter soggy popcorn on the sticky floors of darkened independent cinemas around the country in memory of classic 1980s movie *The Long Good Friday*, which has passed away following news that it is to get a 'Hollywood makeover' from director Paul W. S. Anderson.

The Long Good Friday was born in 1980, the gritty and resolutely unglamorous tale of gangster Harold Shand's attempts to give some legitimacy to his East End criminal empire. Starring Bob Hoskins and Her Majesty Queen Elizabeth II (or possibly Helen Mirren), *The Long Good Friday* was rightly hailed as one of the greatest ever gangster movies, able to stand shoulder-to-shoulder beside Mike Hodges's legendary revenge tale *Get Carter* and brilliant crime-caper *The Italian Job* in the pantheon of British cinema.

This triumvirate would inspire Britons throughout the 1980s, 1990s and noughties to believe that they could create movies capable of standing against Hollywood's best without resorting to long, slow pans across rolling countryside and Kate Winslet in a bosom-flattering Georgian frock, or getting Richard Curtis to write yet another piece of heart-warming drivel about how a floppy-haired, repressed Brit living in a racially-segregated London where it always snows at Christmas can be saved from disaster by the presence of a moderately bankable Hollywood star name.

Yet the mere fact of greatness has never ensured proper recognition. Soon the British gangster movie was not merely inspiring the great and the good but also the not-so-great, the frankly-indifferent and the bloody awful. Where once giants like Harold Shand and Jack Carter had stalked Britain's grimy streets, now they were filled with British bratpackers, desperate to prove their serious acting credentials by dropping the odd aitch and 'giving it large'... and Guy Ritchie.

Such an end would be piteous enough but worse was to come. Concerned by the respect that was still being shown in some quarters to the ageing British threesome, the big boys over in Hollywood decided to send hit men across the pond to sort the trio out. The first to fall was *Get Carter*, mysteriously plunged into a river of bad notices, weighed down by a concrete-shoed performance from Sylvester Stallone. Next came *The Italian Job*, knocked down by a Mini Cooper in a Los Angeles street far from its Milanese home.

Only *The Long Good Friday* was left. Hunted through the streets of London, it was eventually cornered in an East End abattoir, where it was hung from a meat-hook for days, its mangled corpse later being discovered dumped on a Miami Street by the director responsible for such luminous moments of cinema as *Mortal Kombat* and *Resident Evil*.

The Long Good Friday will be buried alongside the rapidly-rotating coffins of *Get Carter* and *The Italian Job*. All three are survived by fond memories of the originals, dreadful remakes and, with any luck, a British version of *Chinatown* set in Somerset starring Justin Lee Collins, its final line 'Forget it Jake, this is Nempnett Thrubwell'.

Lord Reith's Legacy
1938–2007

The Legacy of former Director General of the BBC, John Reith, the belief that the purpose of the British Broadcasting Corporation was to 'inform, educate and entertain', passed away this weekend after suffering an apoplectic fit while reading that the BBC considers itself 'too upmarket'.

Lord Reith's Legacy was born in 1938 when the Director General quit his former BBC home for pastures new, leaving behind him a broadcasting organisation imbued with the, perhaps naive, belief that sometimes people deserve more than they want and that, by producing a broad range of programming including material that might occasionally be in danger of stretching viewers' and listeners' minds and exposing them to new thoughts and ideas, the corporation could perform a great service to the nation.

For decade after decade, Lord Reith's Legacy saw the BBC building its reputation as one of the world's most respected broadcasters, cleaving to such traditional values as tolerance and respect for others and to its belief that the communication of knowledge is a noble goal, while seeking to bind together the whole nation even in the face of war, national disaster and Noel Edmonds.

Year after year the BBC went about its business of informing, educating and entertaining the nation, showering it with the plays of John Osborne, David Hare and Dennis Potter, ground-breaking series like Kenneth Clark's *Civilisation*, the satire of *That Was The Week That Was*, the genius of Morecambe and Wise, popular science programmes like *Tomorrow's World*, innovative and penetrating arts programming, films by Ken Russell, popular dramas from Troy Kennedy Martin, Nigel Kneale et al. And all this in the face of attack from left, right and middle, whether as a 'slave of the establishment' or a 'member of the politically correct subsidariat'.

As the years passed, however, the old lion of broadcasting began to age. As its mane became shaggier and its claws less sharp, so a young rival began to bare its teeth. Roaring out a cry of 'Foul' at the BBC's license-fee funded programming (whilst making no mention of its own ability to cross-fund itself from the profits – barely taxed by any country – of News International) BSkyB leapt in to make its challenge. Bellowing its buzzwords of 'choice' and 'diversity' (and keeping absolutely schtum about 'low quality' or 'expensive subscriptions') it offered a new kind of leadership to the broadcasting pride, a leadership built on the desire to lay one's paws on the largest possible audience, whatever the price.

Unchallenged by a spineless and spavined regulator, Sky's ascendancy was unstoppable. Soon the other channels fell into place, shuffling their documentaries off to the outer boundaries of the schedules, quietly murdering their arts programmes in their sleep, bludgeoning their science programming with voyeuristic tales of freaks masquerading as sensitive explorations of medical problems.

At last, even the BBC itself – Lord Reith's great gift to the nation – was to fall. Beaten into submission by the unceasing attacks of the press, the vindictiveness of a government unable to forget the BBC's temerity in questioning its desire for war in Iraq and a political establishment desperate for Rupert Murdoch's favour, the ageing Corporation at last buckled at the knee and bowed its head. Its concession in an official report that it provided too much *Today* programme and too little Chris Moyles was too heavy a burden for Lord Reith's Legacy to bear: on reading the news, The Legacy was stricken by both a heart attack and the massive electro-magnetic forces generated by Lord Reith himself revolving in his grave.

Lord Reith's Legacy will be buried at All Souls' Church, Langham Place, opposite Broadcasting House. It was predeceased by Foreign Language Films on Terrestrial TV, Intelligent Science Programmes on TV, Original Plays on TV, High-quality Arts Programmes on TV, Probing Celebrity Interviews on TV, Intelligent Documentaries unrelated to the Nazis or Al Qaida on TV and any kind of programming which might – however briefly – force the viewer to do anything beyond sitting slack-jawed on their sofa and letting the last of their atrophied brain cells drool out onto the floor from their limp lips whilst watching Graham Norton scouring the Internet for transsexual Alsatians and alfalfa farmers who dress up as Wonder Woman.

Lord Reith's Legacy is survived by an unmitigated diet of soap operas, cop shows and hospital shows, endless *Big Brother* and Chris Moyles's jackboot stamping on the face of humanity – forever.

The Milkybar Kid

1961–2006

Oversized, sweet-fixated children and lovers of 1970s advertising are today united in mourning The Milkybar Kid, who passed away on Friday.

The Kid, perhaps the only ten-year-old, bespectacled albino ever to make a living in America's Wild West, burst into the nation's consciousness in 1961: a rough, tough, specky cowboy, who would lasso young children and force feed them with his sugary treats – thus providing the inspiration for both *Chitty Chitty Bang Bang*'s Child Catcher and innumerable paedophiles. Despite such questionable behaviour, The Kid and his stunningly banal catchphrase 'The Milkybars are on me!' became an instant hit with the youth of Britain, inspiring millions of boys to spice up their games of 'cowboys and injuns' with fantastically incompetent demonstrations of lasso technique and fragile-family-heirloom-damaging skills.

Times were changing, however, and The Kid was slow to change with them. As a new generation of children began to swap their cap-guns for light sabers (thus affording even greater opportunity for damaging fragile heirlooms) The Kid's spinning-circle-of-rope-based antics began to look increasingly passé. When he did finally make the leap into space his efforts were – as even his closest friends were later to admit – somewhat embarrassing. Deserted by his public, The Kid followed many other one-time stars into obscurity. No longer under pressure to preserve his image, he gave in to his sickly-sweet-chocolate-style-substance obsession, sitting alone at home and mainlining bar after bar. In the following years he fell completely from the media's gaze, save for a brief – balding and bloated – appearance in the tabloids during the early noughties 'paedo' scares, when he was forced to deny ever having asked his old pal the Cadbury's Lad to show him his finger of fudge.

Earlier this year The Kid was admitted to St Ofcom's Hospital where, along with other hawkers of fattening foodstuffs, he underwent a series of investigations. It soon became apparent that he was unfit for the modern age and did not have much longer to live. It came as little surprise when, on Friday, Ofcom doctors announced The Kid's death, which they attributed to a massive overdose of a powdery white substance believed to be sugar.

The Milkybar Kid will be buried in an oversized coffin on Monday. The service will be televised although, under new advertising regulations children will only be able to watch it after the watershed... if their chubby fingers aren't so large that they mash the buttons on the remote control.

Online Poker

2000–2006

Reports of the death of Online Poker have not, it would appear, been exaggerated. The latest bulletins from those checking Online Poker's failing stock market pulse over the last few days confirm that 'OP' – as it was known to its pals – died last night following a surprise attack on Friday by 492 US senators desperately in search of mid-term re-election.

The senators' attack put a brutal end to a life lived on the edge of and beyond the law in the Wild West of the Internet. Born in Britain, after a youth in which it quickly learned how to take candy from babies, OP soon went on to parting fools from their money – preferably thousands of fools from lots and lots of money. Soon it was striding into gathering places across the web offering the chance to lose vast amounts of cash without ever having to enter a seedy bar or meet the men who planned to break your legs.

It was in its success that the seeds of OP's downfall lay. Pious churchmen and even more pious online bookmakers, lottery organisers and Las Vegas casino-owners were driven to condemn the wicked-ways of this dastardly out-of-towner. By the spring of 2006 they had clubbed together to hire the services of one of the most notorious gangs in all of the United States – the Capitol Hill Mob.

The final, fatal attack came on Friday, during a game of draw poker. Having failed to secure its usual seat at the gaming table facing towards the door by means of the usual ~~bribes~~ lobby payments, OP was just reaching forward to rake easy money off another million hopeless losers when it was shot through the back of the head with three bullets from a .45 amendment to the Safe Port Act.

Online Poker is survived by Online Betting on Horse-Races, Online Lotteries and several trillion pages of Internet porn.

Open University Broadcasting

1971–2006

Open University Broadcasting made its last broadcast in the early hours of Saturday morning surrounded by friends and family, including nightshift workers, insomniacs and party-goers on a come-down who were too addled to change the channel.

Conceived at the height of the Summer of Love by Harold Wilson as a 'university of the air', Open University Broadcasting was born on 3 January 1971. It was a precocious and preternaturally gifted child – within seconds of its birth it uttered its first words: 'Welcome to Maths M001: Problems in Practical Calculus.' Almost literally overnight, OU Broadcasting became a firm favourite of a new breed of students and lank-haired, kipper-tied, polyester-shirted hippies who were 'totally blown away by the theme tune, man'.

Throughout the 1970s, OU Broadcasting gave thousands of sartorially-challenged misfits the opportunity to partake in higher education without suffering the embarrassment of actually leaving their homes. In a time when only three channels were available on UK televisions, and before the great cultural leap forward of 24-hour broadcasting, OU Broadcasting provided square-eyed viewers with the chance to stay up past the national anthem and enjoy thrilling night-time programmes such as *History H233:*

Italian Renaissance Cheesecloth Manufacturing, Biology B176: Asexual Reproduction in Milton Keynes and *Polyesterology P034: The Semiology of the Tie in Post-Capitalist Society.*

In the mid 1970s, OU Broadcasting became embroiled in controversy following its decision to broadcast in colour, partly due to the expense of the move but mainly due to the fact so many viewers were stricken blind by the combination of paisley shirts and kipper ties sported by programme presenters, which were so hideous that no man could view them without risking insanity.

By the 1990s the advent of the Internet and DVDs led socially-inept night owls to rely less on OU Broadcasting. Desperate attempts to sustain its academic career with scraps of work for *Coast* and *Lenny's Britain* plunged OU Broadcasting into a deep depression. And it was this, in conjunction with 35 years of late-nights and early mornings, which caused producers to take the decision to pull the plug at 5.30 a.m. on Saturday morning.

Open University Broadcasting was buried in the early morning schedules of BBC2. It was predeceased by Intelligent Science Programmes on British Television and is survived by ITV Play, The Hits, BBC News 24 and the *Big Brother* Live Feed.

Sir Edward Elgar

1857–2007

The news of the death of Sir Edward Elgar will come as an enormous shock to all those who loved him, particularly given that he was born in 1857 and was originally believed to have died in 1934.

Famed throughout his first life for such great works as the *Enigma Variations* and the *Pomp and Circumstance Marches* that gave birth to 'Land of Hope and Glory', Sir Edward Elgar was one of the greatest British composers. Many believe his music had an uncanny ability to connect with the British people, an ability that was doubtless the product both of his enormous (and self-taught) musical gifts and of the fact that he first started composing in earnest while working as bandmaster at the Worcester and County Lunatic Asylum. At the time of his original death in 1934 he was the country's best-loved composer and Master of the King's Musick.

Left to rest peacefully in his grave for more than 65 years, Sir Edward was only exhumed in 1999, when the authorities at the Royal Mint decided to place him on the face of the £20 note – a position from which he could look down on Charles Darwin and his £10 note and look up to Sir John Houblon and his £50 note, doubtless joining the rest of the public in wondering who the hell Sir John Houblon was and what on earth he had done to rank above one of Britain's greatest composers and one of the world's greatest scientists.

For eight years, Sir Edward did loyal service on the £20 note, whether being slid into wallets, crumpled into pockets, rolled up in the lavatories of media haunts and snorted through, or even handed over to politicians in exchange for a 'baronetcy for myself and summink nice for the wife'. Through all the impromptu origami sessions and dark moments on boil wash while lying forgotten in a back pocket, the aged composer uttered no word of complaint.

Despite such Stakhanovite toil, Sir Edward soon found himself the victim of a whispering campaign in the Mint. He was, it was said, too old-fashioned and easy to copy – a charge which was to prove all too true when it was discovered that his image was spending more time on photocopiers than that fat bloke from accounting's arse did at office parties.

Sir Edward's doom was decreed. In March 2007 he was cast aside by the Royal Mint, to be replaced by the great Scottish economist Adam Smith – the man who first felt the invisible hand of the market (though the matter has yet to be brought to court). Sir Edward will be buried in the graveyard of deceased banknote characters alongside Sir Isaac Newton, Charles Dickens, William Shakespeare, Florence Nightingale and that dodgy copy of Elizabeth Fry on a five-pound note I got passed with the rest of my change in the pub last night.

Environment

Branscombe Beach

200 Million BC–AD 2007

Mourners are already gathering to commemorate Branscombe Beach in Devon, which died this week after being poisoned by the cargo ship *MSC Napoli* and trampled to death by freelance 'environmentalists' engaged in a desperate last-ditch 'rescue mission' (their mission being to rescue as much free stuff as possible before the police realised that taking shipwrecked goods without consent is actually theft).

Branscombe Beach began its very long life during the Jurassic Period 200 million years ago when a marine incursion flooded Devon, providing it with its first shale beaches, spectacular cliffs, wonderful sea views and the beginnings of a long history of coastal vandalism.

For most of its life, Branscombe Beach contented itself with lying around and staring peacefully out to sea – its seaside idyll shattered only by the occasional passing teenage ichthyosaur pausing just long enough to leave its fin-print in some fresh shale for posterity.

It was with the arrival of man that Branscombe Beach's life changed forever. Early Neanderthals would gather by the sea in summer to complain that The Beach was pebbly and not sandy, scream at their children, and dream of a day when the sea would bear giant cargo coracles that they could lure to the shore and pillage.

Celtic tribes settled near The Beach around the start of the last millennium but continuous battles over seaside cream-tea franchises are thought to have taken their toll on The Beach. Its health continued to suffer in its later years as hopes of a quiet retirement were further dashed by an influx of smugglers and professional shipwreckers, lighting fires on The Beach and luring unsuspecting ships (and seamen) to their death in the hope of 'salvaging' the latest tricorn hats bound for the Americas, or a BMW coach and four.

The Beach's weakened constitution was dealt a fatal blow when the *MSC Napoli*, bound for South Africa, got into trouble and was deliberately run aground, choking The Beach with fuel oil and the personal possessions of a Swedish family – including their prized collection of Abba albums and a cherished Ikea 'Billy' bookcase that had been in the family for nearly fifteen years.

Branscombe Beach was buried beneath a mountain of twisted freight containers, shattered gear-boxes, nappies and looters who were 'just looking after the motorbike until we can return it to its rightful owner', not to mention a thin veneer of oil, dead marine life and asphyxiated seabirds. The local council has refused permission for a cremation.

The Beach is survived by hundreds of miles of unspoilt Devon coastline – until the next ship disgorges its cargo providing a magnet for thieves from as far away as Middlesborough, desperate to get their hands on an empty barrel or some brine-flavoured cat food.

Cheap Flights

1985–2007

Cheap Flights have reached the end of their short but lucrative runway following the announcement of plans to introduce a tax on frequent flyers with a green air miles scheme designed to limit damage to the environment – particularly if that environment is anywhere in the vicinity of a hen party with £1 tickets to Dublin.

Cheap Flights took off for the first time in 1985 when Ryanair went into competition with British Airways and Aer Lingus, flying from Waterford to London, and providing a much cheaper alternative by economising on 'fancy frills' such as customer service and leg room for anyone taller than the Seven Dwarves.

By the early 1990s Cheap Flights had become a popular and cost-effective way of enjoying what felt like a near-death experience at a fraction of the cost of a day out at Alton Towers. With EU deregulation of the air industry in 1997, the skies over Britain were filled with planes carrying passengers to weekends in such romantic European destinations as Stuttgart, that strange bit of Paris that is actually 50 miles from the city itself and is only used by low-cost airlines and the crop-dusting plane from *North by Northwest,* and the Stansted Travelodges that are the only alternative when you've been unexpectedly bumped off a flight despite having booked it several months in advance.

With growing concern over the environmental impact of low-cost airlines during the noughties, the twenty-first century equivalent of the Battle of Britain began. In the early days of

113

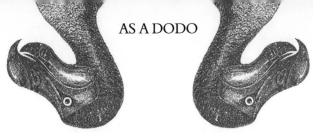

the conflict, Ryanair and easyJet prevailed but, despite increased demand for short-haul flights (so-called because the passengers were often called upon to haul the plane from the terminal concourse to the runway), environmentally-aware politicians and Conservatives looking for an image change soon began to inflict heavy losses.

The last post was sounded when Shadow Chancellor George Osborne dared to speak out – his voice hardly breaking at all – on behalf of the environment, in a brave move intended to protect our beautiful planet and in no way connected with the opportunity to embarrass a Labour government with all the green credentials of Jeremy Clarkson.

When David Cameron – who had joined the mile high club as a teenager despite never having boarded a plane – came flying out of the sun with all environmental policies blazing, Cheap Flights were riddled with holes, took a sudden nose-dive and crashed and burned... something many passengers had been predicting would happen for years.

Cheap Flights will be buried at St Leslie Nielsen's Church of *Airplane!* Mourners will be flown to East Midlands Airport, 120 miles from the service held in the duty-free concourse of Luton Airport. Admission will be 50p (including wake taxes £75) plus a 100 cl bottle of Lithuanian red wine (£4) and complementary nuts at £12.50. Passengers will be asked to join in the singing of Cheap Flights' favourite hymn 'There is an Airport Far Away'.

Cheap Flights are survived by unseasonably warm weather, a load of lonely raffia donkeys and a massive increase in dayglo fake tans.

The Chelsea Tractor
1941–2006

Middle-class West London mums and Jeremy Clarkson have been united in mourning the untimely death of The Chelsea Tractor, '4x4', 'SUV' or '4WD': the powerful beasts that once roamed roads across the globe and which, for many, came to epitomise strength, versatility and total disregard for the environment.

First sighted in the wild in the early 1940s and then known as 'Jeeps', Chelsea Tractors were initially feral creatures, given to scrambling up hillsides and along twisting jungle paths and frequently involved in scenes of battle during World War Two, or outside Loretta Switt's trailer in *M*A*S*H* that time Alan Alda accidentally drove over her foot.

Some of the first attempts to tame the Jeep were made in Britain. A careful programme of cross-breeding resulted in the production of the 'Land Rover', a sturdy (if usually slow) creature that spent its time skittering up mountainsides and down into valleys from the Scottish Highlands to the Cornish Coast, usually with a sheep or two in the back and a lonely shepherd in a mounting state of excitement in the front.

By the late 1960s and early 1970s, the rugged 4x4s were a familiar sight across the countryside and even occasionally on the outskirts of towns and cities. But as their favourite foodstuff grew scarce during the oil crisis of 1973, many predicted the powerful, if sometimes ungainly, animals could go the way of the dodo. They were, however, able to survive in isolated rural pockets, living off a diet of red diesel and the odd drop of four-star.

With the species' very survival under threat, top scientists at car manufacturers in America, Europe and Japan began selective breeding programmes. By the mid 1980s the first Chelsea Tractors were released into a new, safe environment – the city. Soon Chelsea Tractors were swarming over smog-filled traffic routes in urban centres the world over, braving hazards from speed bumps up to 5 cm high all the way to potholes up to 2 cm deep in their quest to deliver little Julian safely to soccer practice.

It was not long before predators began to gather. Soon groups of environmental activists, teenagers eager for a cause and politicians eager to sweep up the green vote were seen gathering near the Chelsea Tractors' watering holes ('petrol stations') and sniffing the air, before passing out due to all the fumes. Before long they took to setting up traps for the turbo-powered behemoths in the form of congestion charges and by poisoning their food supply with green taxes.

By the mid-noughties, the Chelsea Tractor was vanishing from our streets. By the end there were only a few, unreliable sightings of the creatures – sometimes outside the palatial crib of an LA rapper, sometimes making the weary journey to Knightsbridge for the sales.

The Chelsea Tractor will be buried under a mountain of high petrol prices and increased environmental awareness. It is survived by an increasing number of erratic cyclists, scooters, bendy buses, the Smart car and trees.

Rapid Global Warming
1979–2007

The death of Rapid Global Warming was received with scenes of joyous celebration around the world when it was announced that President George W. Bush – inspired by the brilliant work of Montgomery Burns and Professor Ogden Wernstrom – had authorised a crack squad of highly-trained giant mirrors to assassinate it by cutting off its vital supply of light from the sun.

Rapid Global Warming was born in 1979 to a long line of Warmings which have ruled the planet since time immemorial. The youngest Warming quickly set to work in the family business and soon made its parents proud as it increased the rate of land temperature twice as fast as ocean temperatures. Setting a pace faster than any predecessor since that embarrassing incident with the barbie led to the Paleocene-Eocene Thermal Maximum, many critics alleged that it was only able to maintain itself by mainlining fossil fuels in quantities that would make even Keith Richards wobble slightly and go, 'Wow!'

Throughout the 1980s and 1990s, Rapid Global Warming was engaged in a long battle against opponents such as The Greens, riding roughshod over claims that its fossil fuel intake would lead to the destruction of the planet and breaking into their house at night while they were sleeping, to leave their TV, stereo and PC on standby and leave their fridge door open.

It was in the early twenty-first century that the first blow against Rapid Global Warming was struck, when the US government, realising that invading foreign countries for oil is a lot more trouble than it's worth, rushed to staunch its haemorrhaging popularity by launching a sneak attack using the most-sophisticated sun-blocking technology since the invention of the knotted handkerchief. Crippled by the most cunning plan in space since the cool-headed and logical thinking which gave birth to President Reagan's *Star Wars* laser-missile defence plan, Rapid Global Warming quickly fell into decline. It finally passed away at the weekend at its family home, with all the windows open and the radiators on full blast.

Rapid Global Warming will be cremated on top of a giant oil well at St Bush's Church of Last-Ditch Idiotic Ideas. It is survived by the US government's plan to save us all by launching giant mirrors into space to block sunlight from reaching the Earth, and an increased use of fossil fuels and nuclear power to meet the giant surge in demand for electricity as we try to see just where the hell we're going and what the f**k we're doing during the long, dark days of the coming ice age.

The Turkey

10 Million BC–AD the Last Thursday in November

The Turkey, the bird that has – since the collapse of the bald eagle population and the ascendancy of the Bush dynasty – come to symbolise the United States in so many ways, was assassinated on the last Thursday in November on a vast array of dining tables across the North American continent. Police say they were powerless to prevent the turkeycide, despite having prior knowledge of the plot.

The Turkey was born into the family *Meleagris gallopavo* 10 million years ago and quickly established itself throughout considerable parts of North America. It was not until the latter part of its long life that The Turkey first made its mark upon American society, when it established a trading relationship with Native Americans. They provided The Turkey with somewhere extremely warm to roost and The Turkey returned the favour by providing them with food, flights for arrows and feathers for headdresses.

It was with the arrival of the Pilgrim Fathers in 1620 that The Turkey began its meteoric rise to stardom. A year later, the surviving pilgrims celebrated a successful harvest with their new friend The Turkey and gave thanks that they were no longer living in England – a tradition which millions of grateful Americans continue to this day.

In later years, The Turkey became a presidential favourite. Abraham Lincoln honoured it with its own annual public holiday, Thanksgiving, where families gathered together to offer thanks to The Turkey for being such a great pal and going so well with candied yams. This was far from the last honour the bird was to receive: in 1947 Harry S. Truman instituted the practice of giving The Turkey a presidential pardon – a tradition for which Richard Nixon was later to be extremely grateful.

The Turkey became the first bird on the Moon, sharing a meal with Neil Armstrong and Buzz Aldrin. However, Aldrin has never forgiven NASA for selecting Armstrong to open his foil food first, while Armstrong has never lived down his famous slip of the tongue, 'Houston, The Turkey has landed.'

In 2000 The Turkey had its finest hour when it was elected forty-third president of the United States. But the once popular bird soon began to lose its loyal following when it stopped talking turkey and became mired in a series of political scandals which many believe led to the brutal slaying of The Turkey by a lone assailant and 300 million accomplices.

The Turkey was cremated in a slow and moving ceremony, spoilt only by a large family row about who knocked over the gravy boat. In attendance were its close friends Stuffing, Mashed Potatoes, Sweet Potatoes, Cranberry Sauce, Succotash and Pumpkin Pie.

The Turkey is survived by the music of Paris Hilton and the movies of Rob Schneider.

Weekly Rubbish Collection

*c.*500 BC–AD 2007

People throughout the country are today putting pegs on their noses and dragging out their pomanders as they prepare to remember the sweet(ish)-smelling streets of England that existed before the death of Weekly Rubbish Collection, which has passed away across much of the realm.

Weekly Rubbish Collection was born in Athens in about 500 BC, when the sudden outbreak of democracy finally allowed the people of the city state a chance to complain about the huge pile of rubbish that had been building up for the past few hundred years without fear of one of the tyrant's hoplites gently counselling them at spear-point to 'shut up and get back to the philosophising'.

Despite numerous advances in waste technology by the Romans, the progress of rubbish collection was halted and then put into reverse by the arrival of the Dark Ages, so-called presumably because no one wanted to put a light on for fear of seeing the great piles of ordure that surrounded them.

In 1354 Weekly Rubbish Collection finally came to Britain, with each of London's wards employing 'muckrakers' to rake rubbish together, load it into carts and remove it once a week (unlike today, when muckrakers rake rubbish together, load it into their laptops and publish it in newspapers and on the Internet every day).

The glory days of Weekly Rubbish Collection, however, were ushered in by the Industrial Revolution. With the streets now filled with malodorous waste and malodorous freelance waste-collectors, in 1875 The Public Health Act was passed, requiring local authorities to arrange the removal and disposal of waste and requiring householders to store their rubbish in dustbins.

For more than a hundred years the system worked well. Each week the dustbin men would arrive at an ungodly hour in the morning and rouse the sleeping neighbourhood with an impromptu rendition of the louder bits of *Stomp*, before collecting up the rubbish bins and scattering a portion of their contents over the streets as an offering to the dusty gods.

But with new technologies and increasing wealth – not to mention supermarkets' desire to add value to their products by encasing them in more packaging than is required for the disposal of nuclear waste – came an explosion in the amount of rubbish generated by each household. Soon landfill sites were filling up and incinerators were overloading. In the end the only option was to cancel Weekly Rubbish Collection altogether, replacing it with its younger sibling Alternate Weekly Collection, which merrily collected rubbish one week and recycling the next – leaving the rest to hang around attracting flies, rats and tabloid hacks desperate for a scoop about what Z-list celebrities throw away.

Weekly Rubbish Collection was cremated in a municipal incinerator before having its ashes scattered up and down the street outside your front door. It is survived by a surprisingly fat urban fox population, piles of bin bags on the pavement and a continuing unwillingness on the part of Brits to recycle rubbish anywhere other than their TV screens.

The White Cliffs of Dover

*c.*10,000 BC–AD 2007

There are no more bluebirds over The White Cliffs of Dover, that ancient symbol of this sceptred isle which has – to judge by the media reports at the time – crumbled and sunk beneath the English Channel following the complete destruction of Kent, and everyone in it, during a massive earthquake on Saturday morning.

The White Cliffs of Dover were born 12,000 years ago as the Ice Age ended and the melting glaciers exposed the chalk edifices in their full, pasty glory for the first time. Within days, The Cliffs became a rallying point for patriotically-minded hunter-gatherers unnaturally proud of their new island status, sending out a message of British independence to those pesky Gauls across the Channel – not to mention becoming a popular jumping-off point for effete *Guardian*-reading hunter-gatherers who had already grown weary of patriotically-minded hunter-gatherers' intolerance towards their European neighbours.

Over the centuries The Cliffs guarded the gateway to Britain, warning off invaders from Napoleon to Hitler who schemed to add this green ~~and pleasant~~ land to their empire of subjugated territories, and completely failing to halt those invaders like Julius Caesar and William the Conqueror who had the nous to land at more gently-sloping beaches further along the coast.

Sadly, excessive performances by Vera Lynn during World War Two took their toll on The Cliffs and they lacked the strength to raise two fingers to the continent. In the late twentieth century, giant machines bored a huge tunnel through The Cliffs' heart, allowing millions of tourists to travel at high-speeds to London and thousands of desperate refugees dreaming of a better life to take up those really crappy jobs that Britons themselves refused to touch with a barge pole – much to the outrage of those very same Britons who kept complaining loudly about 'these bloody people coming over here' even as they purchased their burgers from them, got them to fix their dodgy sewerage systems and sent them out to drown whilst cockle-picking.

Fatally undermined, The Cliffs stood no chance against the powerful earthquake measuring a massive 4.3 on the Richter scale (about the equivalent of two bluebirds colliding) which struck in the Straits of Dover in 2007. Panic ensued as Canterbury Cathedral collapsed (its extensive building insurance failing to protect it from an act of God), the people of Tunbridge Wells were buried under an avalanche of disgusted letters to the *Daily Mail* about the incorrect use of the word 'whom' and the town of Sandwich's plan to shelter itself between two layers of bread proved a complete and utter failure. Kent slid into the English Channel and the Garden of England became the Sunken Garden of England, The White Cliffs of Dover hanging on until the very end when even they were submerged beneath the churning grey water and buried at sea, along with the last vestiges of Britain's insular and arrogant attitude towards the rest of Europe and everyone in it. But still… at least we're now a lot further away from the French.

International Politics

Bush and Blair

2001–2007

Comedy fans are mourning the death of one of the world's funniest double acts, Bush and Blair, following the shock announcement by British Prime Minister Tony Blair that he has decided to withdraw from his comic partnership with the US President George Bush and will no longer be joining him on the set of the latest in their series of hilarious *Road to* movies, *The Road to a New Vietnam*.

It was in 2001 that Tony Blair decided to replace his former sidekick Bill 'Slick Willie' Clinton after Clinton's comic persona as a loveable Lothario – and catchphrase 'I did not have sexual relations with that woman' – began to prove box-office death in America's post-millennial moral climate. Initially Blair had hoped to hook up with Clinton's old straight man, Al Gore, but opted instead for the guy behind the tongue-tied goof routine that stole American hearts – and votes – during the 2000 Presidential Election.

Almost immediately Bush and Blair began preparations for their hilariously titled 'Bringing Democracy' world tour, Blair spending each day working on the wonderfully ludicrous 'I'm a Pretty Straight Kinda Guy' routine that had won him the laughter of audiences across the UK, while Dubya perfected everything from his 'Kenny Boy Lay? Never Met Him In My Life' skit to the death-defying piece of physical comedy that was 'Chewing A Pretzel'.

With Bush and Blair's comic characters in place, Dubya playing a knuckle-dragging jock and Blair the smooth-talking poodle that insisted on following him everywhere he went, Bush's long-time manager Dick Cheney spotted the box-office potential in the sequence of scripts that would become the pair's *Road to* movies. Soon they were laughing on *The Road to Democracy*, sweeping along the dusty *Road to Afghan Liberation* and crying on *The Road to Iraqi Freedom* (known in the UK under the title *The Road to Electoral Suicide*).

It was during the filming of the last of these three movies that rumours of a split first surfaced. Crew members reported the sounds of heated arguments emerging from the pair's trailer and more and more often the once inseparable duo were seen to arrive and leave the set apart. The cause, some claim, was the latest script optioned for the pair by Mr Cheney, *The Road to Iran* (also known as *The Road to Armageddon*). Whatever the basis for the dispute, it was increasingly clear that relations between the two men had begun to sour. Indeed, it came as little surprise when, Mr Blair announced he was pulling out of the duo's latest Iraq tour, 'The Big Troop Surge', to concentrate on other projects.

The comedy duo that was Bush and Blair will be remembered fondly by its fans, both of whom can be found in a secure wing of The Charge of the Light Brigade Hospital for the Militarily Insane.

Bush and Blair are now working on their solo projects: Tony Blair's 'Legacy Tour' and George Bush's 'Who Gives A Crap? I Ain't Standing For Election Again' stand-up appearances in Washington's premier comedy venue, the White House.

The Death of the Cold War
1989–2007

The Death of the Cold War died last night when MPs voted by a majority of 248 to renew Britain's Trident nuclear submarines, thus bringing the country kicking and screaming into the 1950s, prepared at any moment to deter the threat of a massive nuclear attack by the forces of the USSR, the Eastern Bloc and Red China with the prospect of mutually assured destruction, despite the fact that the USSR no longer exists, the Eastern Bloc's forces are already working over here as plumbers and the biggest invasion threat from China is from an influx of extremely cheap T-shirts.

The Death of the Cold War began in 1989 with the fall of the Berlin Wall which left that once divided city vulnerable to unscrupulous capitalists determined to (literally) smash communism – charging $10 a throw for a piece of grafittied rubble and leaving the city wide open to the horror of an invading army of Pink Floyd fans.

Soon Eastern Bloc countries – sick of suffering under communist oppression and the occasional visit by Sir Paul McCartney – were demanding the right to elect democratic governments, hold their own concerts featuring 1970s rock dinosaurs, eat quarter-pounders with cheese and yearn for the days of communist oppression.

Thanks to The Death, a generation raised on Cold War paranoia – including *Invasion of the Body Snatchers*, *When the Wind Blows* and *Red Dawn* – breathed a sigh of relief as the superpowers stepped back from the brink of nuclear annihilation. At last ordinary

citizens could rest safe in the knowledge that the man in the park whispering 'the red squirrel flies low over the Volga tonight' wasn't a Soviet agent, but an alternative comedian filming an ironic lager commercial.

All seemed well until, urged on by our Great Leader Comrade Brown and his predecessor Comrade Blair, Britain chose to follow the examples of Iran and North Korea and commission new nuclear weapons to prove to the world that, for all it seems to be a crumbling state unable even to care for the health of its people, it is in truth a powerful player on the global stage. The Great Leader's success was due in no small part to the support of opposition leader Comrade Cameron, who also requested that all new missiles be fitted with windmills so they can generate gigawatts of environmentally-friendly electricity as they hurtle towards Minsk at several thousand miles per hour.

The Death of the Cold War will be buried on May Day at Whitehall at a ceremony witnessed by Comrade Brown, who will stand on the newly erected balcony at 10 Downing Street, smile grimly beneath his Homburg, and stiffly salute a march-past of the missiles of the Glorious People's Republic of Britain... before personally executing the 95 Labour rebels who voted against him.

It is survived by the four-minute warning and shooting your irradiated grandmother with a 12-bore to stop her getting her crazed, mutated hands on your last tin of Alphabetti Spaghetti.

Donald Rumsfeld's Political Career

1957–2006

The Political Career of Donald Henry Rumsfeld died last night, shortly after a large group of Washington villagers carrying pitchforks and torches arrived outside the White House demanding that President Bush 'destroy the monster'.

Donald Rumsfeld's Political Career came into its own in 1969 when – following an accident in which Donald was fatally injured by the explosion of his own over-inflated ego – Rumsfeld was reconstructed in a secret lab in the Chicago School of Economics. The creature that emerged from that laboratory was hailed as a new Adam by its neoconservative creators, a sin against nature by its opponents and '… a ruthless little bastard, you can be sure of that' by its new employer, President Nixon.

When Nixon was forced out of the White House as one of the most reviled leaders of the US since King George, it came as little surprise that Mr Rumsfeld's unique talents were recognised by another great statesman, President Gerald Ford, who made Donald the youngest ever Secretary of Defense. In 1977 President Ford awarded Mr Rumsfeld the Presidential Medal of Freedom. By 1978 Mr Ford had lost an election.

In the next few years The Political Career largely lay dormant, satisfying its unnatural urges by supplying Saddam Hussein with weaponry and intelligence under President Reagan and selling nuclear equipment to North Korea in accord with the wishes of the Clinton administration.

In 2000 Mr Rumsfeld was selected for service by George W. Bush. By 2001 he was in charge of the Department of Defense once more. His success in transforming the military – despite opposition from the dinosaurs at the Pentagon – into a 'light and nimble' force was seen in 2003 when the invasion and pacification of Iraq was carried out by Sergeant Dwight Shergenhauer armed only with a spoon. Sadly, Mr Rumsfeld's prediction that the people of Iraq would all spontaneously lay down their arms and burst into hymns of praise for George W. Bush and the American way were ruined by the liberal media, the ungrateful families of dead servicemen and those same dinosaur generals at the Pentagon.

As the war became increasingly unpopular, The Political Career was seen stalking the Department of Defense, committing random appalling acts such as using a machine to sign letters of condolence, torturing the English language during press conferences and remaining in its post after the Abu Ghraib scandal. With opinion among the public turning against it, The Political Career was ultimately to end its days by plunging from the roof of the Pentagon. Those first at the scene – Dick Cheney, Karl Rove and George W. Bush – all confirm that the death was definitely suicide.

Donald Rumsfeld's Political Career will be buried in a series of lucrative company directorships. It is survived by the knowledge that, with Mr Rumsfeld no longer in charge of America's military, the Rapture is just that little bit further away.

The Eighth Amendment to the US Constitution

1789–2006

People across the globe are holding candlelit vigils today in memory of The Eighth Amendment to the US Constitution, which has died at the age of 217 following an unfortunate incident last night involving Vice President Dick Cheney and a large body of water.

Born in 1789 to the Enlightenment and the founding fathers, as a child The Eighth Amendment was a robust and forthright article of the US Bill of Rights, preventing the infliction of cruel and unusual punishment. Its birth was hailed by freedom-loving peoples across the globe and utterly condemned by torturers, members of the Honourable Guild of Racksmiths and Thumbscrewwrights, and dentists.

As it grew, The Eighth Amendment stuck to its campaigning path, successfully outlawing drawing and quartering, public dissecting, burning alive and disembowelling, thus helping to maintain the reputation of the US as a bastion of freedom as well as putting a severe crimp on the kind of programmes they can show on the Fox Network. Not all was to go well for The Amendment, however. By the twentieth century increasing concern was being shown over its behaviour, especially after the discovery of a large collection of really-rather-cruel-and-unusual-seeming equipment for lethal injections, gas chambers and electric chairs was discovered in its back yard. Claims that these were reserved for ceremonial use by state governors seeking the US presidency were dismissed, especially after it was revealed that The Eighth Amendment was offering two-for-one discounts on lethal injections to Texas and was considering a 'frequent fryer' scheme for the state of Nebraska.

Despite such questions, The Eighth Amendment was still respected across the globe until the early part of the twenty-first century, when it suddenly went missing one night after being seen in the company of a balding, white-haired man known to officials only as 'Der Weisse Engel' or the 'forty-sixth vice president of the United States'. Reports of what happened thereafter become unclear, although some claim to have witnessed The Amendment being bundled onto a secret rendition flight to an unnamed ~~torture chamber~~ idyllic village in Eastern Europe. White House sources, in contrast, insist it had merely gone to stay with its close Uzbek relative Vlotar 'Electrodes Up the Jacksie' Tezticklztampuh. In any event it is understood that it was during this trip that The Amendment chose to go for an early morning swim in company with Vice President Cheney, a large board and several straps. Never a strong swimmer, The Amendment fell into difficulty and drowned, despite Mr Cheney's heroic efforts to save it by holding a cloth over its face and repeatedly demanding 'Is it safe?'

The Eighth Amendment to the US Constitution will be quietly buried in an unmarked grave somewhere you've never heard of. Anyone wishing to attend the funeral is asked to wear a hood and orange jumpsuit and be prepared for a long flight.

Enemies of the Russian State

Various Dates–2006

We at As a Dodo *are grateful to our Russian correspondent (appointed only this weekend, after entering our offices bearing a sinister smile, and a large tin of thallium) for the following obituary, which we typed at sushi-point this morning.*

Following the tragic and wholly accidental thallium poisoning of former KGB colonel and present critic of President Putin, Alexander Litvinenko, Enemies of the Russian State are advised that they have now been officially reclassified by the KGB's successor, the Federal'naya Sluzhba Bezopasnosti Rossiyskoi Federatsii (FSB) as dead, and are requested to make the necessary arrangements for their funerals, which will be held on dates to be specified by the shadowy figures they may have noticed loitering near their houses or observing them from behind copies of Pravda over the past few weeks.

Born on various dates, Enemies of the Russian State have a long and ignoble history. In their time they have committed innumerable crimes, among them criticising the Russian state, hinting that bribery and corruption may be a way of life in modern Russia, failing to pay the proper bribes to corrupt Russian officials, being journalists, inquiring too deeply into the actions of the glorious Russian government after being gently advised at Kalashnikov-point that such actions were unwise and looking at President Putin without the officially approved expression of deep love and awe upon their faces.

Since carrying out these heinous acts, Enemies of the Russian State have been declared dead, despite carrying out such life-associated activities as breathing, walking about, talking to their friends and such like. FSB doctors advise that, should these people fail to take vital remedial action – such as acknowledging that President Putin is the surpassing genius of his age whose word is as that of God and whose followers can do no wrong – it is highly likely that their deaths will be confirmed in the following months by accidentally falling off high buildings, throwing themselves in front of speeding vehicles, stabbing themselves with ricin-tipped umbrellas or chopping their own heads off after beating themselves to a pulp.

Enemies of the Russian State will be buried secretly deep in the woods after having their teeth and hands removed to avoid identification. They will not be mourned by anyone living who wishes to remain in that state.

(Fictional) George W. Bush
1946–2006

Many of our readers will be aware of the deep distress caused in the US by Channel 4's Death of a President *which purported to dramatise the effects of the assassination of President Bush. Given the outpouring of grief occasioned by this fictional death, we can only conclude that the American people had confused their real president with another, fictional, president – whose obituary we supply below.*

(Fictional) George W. Bush was born in 1946 into an old, established New England family. Despite the advantages afforded to him by his upbringing, young (Fictional) George preferred not to rely on his patrician background, keen instead to get on in life by hard work and the application of his keen intelligence. It was these qualities that led him to Yale, from where he would graduate cum laude in 1968. Despite his academic brilliance, (Fictional) George was ever eager to serve his country and, despite his misgivings about the conflict in Vietnam, immediately enlisted in the armed forces, ready and willing to serve on the front line.

Returning from war after several tours of duty and having refused all military honours – including the Purple Heart – despite his heroic service, (Fictional) George quickly set himself to work on home territory. Wanting to avoid the feckless life of booze and drugs so common among the scions of America's ruling families and raring to make his own way in the world, (Fictional) George chose not to accept repeated offers from his father's friends in the oil industry, instead choosing to put his deep scientific knowledge to good use by setting up a self-funded environmental technology company. It was, of course, the invention by that same company of the (Fictional) George W. 'Hydropower I' motor that led to the abandonment of hydrocarbon-burning engines in the automobile industry.

Despite the heavy pressures on his time caused by his scientific and environmental work, (Fictional) George was still insistent he had more to do. In 1994 he stood for and was elected Governor of Texas. Few Texans will forget his many successes in that role, including vast reductions in pollution, enormous improvements in educational standards for rich and poor alike, a massive fall in the state's prison population and the near-eradication of poverty. All this while displaying such probity that he insisted on refusing the blandishments of lobbyists and such local favourites as Enron's Kenneth 'Kenny Boy' Lay.

Given his astounding achievements it was certain from the moment he was reluctantly persuaded to stand that (Fictional) George would become president of the United States in the year 2000. His record-breaking 50-state victory was made all the more remarkable by his decision to persuade brother Jeb Bush to stand down as Governor of Florida for the duration of the election, in order to avoid even the suggestion of any possible impropriety. Truly he was the man to bring a new light to the new millennium.

The achievements of (Fictional) President George W. Bush while in office are, needless to say, too numerous to mention. His farsighted choice to bring all his efforts to bear on the resolution of the Middle East conflict, combined with his decision to resist all those who called for an attack on Iraq following the terrible events of 9/11 and concentrate instead on the reconstruction of Afghanistan, undoubtedly contributed to the stability and peace the whole region enjoys today – especially following the capture of Osama bin Laden in 2003 by a US Special Forces group led by (Fictional) George himself.

Thanks to (Fictional) George's tireless championing of the Kyoto Agreement, his commitment to the sciences, leadership on the eradication of poverty throughout the globe and his belief in using America's might only with the greatest of care and planning, it came as no surprise when, earlier this year, the (Fictional) president was awarded the Nobel prizes for physics, chemistry, medicine, economics and peace. Indeed, many had expected him to complete the clean sweep next year, winning the prize for literature with his moving novel based on the life of a poor black man struggling to rebuild his life after the destruction of home and family by Hurricane Katrina.

(Fictional) George W. Bush will be buried on 9 October. A world will mourn.

French Presidential Elections
2007–2007

The As a Dodo *editorial staff would like to thank the eminent* philosophe, *Jacques Derigueur, for penning the following obituary. Sadly, having read the piece, we feel unable to do so.*

Ah oui. Today *la belle* Marianne, symbol of our great country, lies back in her bed, exhausted, satiated, as she ponders the deep mystery that has passed between her and the French Presidential Elections.

Where did it all begin? Let me, like Proust, savour for a moment a tea-soaked morsel of madeleine and be invaded by the sudden pleasure of memory. It was but a few weeks ago that Marianne found herself in peril. While perfidious John Bull sunned himself in the light of his economic stability, poor Marianne was left to skulk in the shade, afflicted by high unemployment and sporadic rioting, consoled only by her appallingly high living standards, superb health service, thriving intellectual culture, excellent education system not yet wholly devoted to utilitarian ends and her football team capable of reaching World Cup finals.

Can we be surprised that Marianne was feeling a certain ennui? Oh yes, she had a lover, but Jacques Chirac was no longer the smooth-talking former mayor of Paris with a devilish look in his eye and an impressively large amount of funds in his pocket. Now he was bent by age and no longer capable of satisfying Marianne's needs. What could she do but look elsewhere?

Soon she found herself being courted day and night by her would-be lovers. Swiftly she rejected the attentions of Jean Marie Le Pen, having tired of his far-right ways during their last dalliance in 2002. Next she refused the protestations of desire from stolid centrist farmer François Bayrou... largely due to his being so boring that she continually fell asleep while he stolidly made love to her.

And so the people of France waited with bated breath as Marianne was forced to choose between her two remaining suitors: the dashing Nicolas Sarkozy, eager to open Marianne's eyes to the dark and sensual pleasures to be found in fiscal fetters and a firm hand, and the striking Ségolène Royal, keen to spend her way to Marianne's heart. Unable to bear the thought of her new love not being able to get half-way through a treaty-signing without all the assembled French men attempting to pinch her bottom, Marianne had no alternative but to reject Ms Royal and settle down to make love, *tout fou*, *tout passionné* with M Sarkozy and his mighty water cannon.

And so, my English friends, the deed is done and *Les Elections Présidentielles Françaises* 2007 have passed away. Marianne has her new lover and only one question remains: who will be doing the screwing and who will get screwed?

The As a Dodo *editors add: The French Presidential Elections 2007 will be buried, along with Jacques Chirac's Political Career, just as soon as the funeral cortège can make it through the traffic jam at the Arc de Triomphe and the attendees end their strike calling for increased crematorium regulation.*

The Iran Hostage Crisis
23 March 2007–5 April 2007

We at As a Dodo *wish to apologise for the following obituary. We recognise that entrusting it to our religious correspondent may have been an error, especially at Easter time when his blood sugar was pumped up on hot cross buns and Easter eggs.*

Now the feast of Passover drew nigh, as did the anniversary of the birth of the Prophet and of the crucifixion of the Lord and the feast of the giant chocolate eggs, when the Thorntonites do celebrate their profit-spike and do fail to apologise for pronouncing 'chocolatier' to rhyme with 'musketeer'.

And lo, 15 men and women of the British Royal Navy did sail upon the waters of the Gulf, where they did carry out a UN mandated patrol. And while they were patrolling upon the waters a force of Iranians did come among them and did seize them, saying that the waters upon which they patrolled were the waters of Iran, whatever their GPS might say. And so the 15 did go with them, for they had had no training as to what to do in such circumstances save for a 20-minute videotape advising them 'not to do anything stupid'.

And so the 15 were taken unto Tehran where they were sore afflicted, being forced to wear ill-fitting Iranian

141

suits and to play chess and smoke cigarettes and lark about a bit for the cameras.

And lo there was a voice crying in the wilderness, which is Texas, and that voice did cry 'That ain't no way to conduct a snatch operation! Thou shouldst have seized the sailors and placed them in garments of orange and bound their hands and gagged their mouths and hooded their heads. And verily thou shouldst then have rendered them up unto the tender mercies of inquisitors in Egypt or Eastern Europe where the inquisitors might smite them about the head and the body and might attach electrodes to their testicles and set dogs upon them and then baptise them for many minutes at a time, until they do admit whatsoever sins the inquisitors may counsel them, in their mercy, to admit. That is what thou shouldst have done with these enemy combatants for that is what I would have done'.

But the lone voice went unheeded and instead there was a wailing and a gnashing of teeth at the viciousness of the conduct of the Iranians towards their captives. And there was a general feeling among the people of America and Britain that they would have acted much better, despite all the evidence that they wouldn't.

And lo, upon the thirteenth day the president of Iran, who is Ahmadinejad, and who does believe himself to be an instrument of the Lord most high, in which he is like unto the president of America and the prime minister of Britain, did go unto the peoples of the press. And Ahmadinejad did speak unto the peoples of the press, saying 'And lo! Now is a really good time for me to get some great publicity for myself after doing unto the economy of my nation what the peoples of Sodom and Gomorrah didst unto each other and unto their sheep and their goats. And lo, as a show of good will towards the British people and some great PR for myself, I shall release these sailors'.

And all the people did cry out saying 'Yes, release them', save for one voice that did cry 'No, welease Bwian', but the people mocked him, for he was a Pythonite.

And so it came to pass that the 15 were made to appear before the president and shake his hand and thank him for his kindness and then they were returned unto Britain, where they were hailed in a manner like unto the Lord coming into Jerusalem on the back of an ass before being crucified by the papers a few days later, for the British press are a wicked people who shall do anything for a headline.

The As a Dodo *editors add: The Iran Hostage Crisis will be buried under a large pile of newsprint and a lengthy inquiry into GPS readings. It is survived by a very self-satisfied Iranian president.*

The Last Possible Reason for War with Iraq

2002–2006

Following the release of hitherto secret files in the US, *As a Dodo* can reveal that the Last Possible Reason for War with Iraq was terminated with extreme prejudice by the CIA last summer and secretly buried by the Bush administration.

The Last Possible Reason for War with Iraq was born to George Bush and Tony Blair in 2002, the youngest of several older Reasons for War with Iraq, including Weapons of Mass Destruction, Control of the Oil Supply and 'Cos it Looked at My Pint Funny, all of which had tragically died in early childhood. Despite this distressing background, The Last Possible Reason refused to be deterred and, within months of its birth, it was leading American troops into war with a smile on its lips, a song in its heart and a wild and wholly false battle cry claiming that Saddam Hussein was linked to Al Qaida bellowing from its throat. Soon it was setting about its multiple tasks of distracting from the search for Osama bin Laden, alienating Islamic opinion and avenging the President's Pa with relish.

In the following years The Last Possibile Reason was to distinguish itself repeatedly in action against senate committees, the international intelligence community and common sense, repeatedly leaping to the lips of such luminaries as Colin Powell, Dick Cheney, Donald Rumsfeld and, of course, the president himself, not to mention all employees of Fox News. Soon it became the rallying call of all those who supported the war in Iraq (from the safety of a sofa in America), enabling them to join together in building some of the greatest achievements of the early twenty-first century, including the removal of civil liberties, increased surveillance of citizenry, heightened paranoia and the abandonment of the norms created by international law and the Geneva Conventions. Despite these successes, however, The Last Possibile Reason was ultimately to fall in the summer of 2005 when, faced with multiple enquiries it was ultimately outgunned by the forces of the truth. Given its many sacrifices, it is perhaps little surprise that despite its defeat, its words are still to be found on the lips of the president almost daily.

The Last Possibile Reason is survived by Dick Cheney, Donald Rumsfeld and a reinvigorated Iran.

NATO

1949–2006

Fans across the globe are mourning the death of NATO, the supergroup that has rocked much of the globe since its foundation in 1949. Brought together from some of the leading powers of the Western world, and Canada, the band was soon building a powerful reputation as it played gigs across much of Western Europe, picking up new members on its travels.

All seemed to be going well until France – angered at what it saw as the US and the UK hogging the limelight – split from the group in the 1960s, intent on pursuing solo projects including Gaullist Arrogance and Building Nuclear Bombs. Despite this the other NATO members soldiered on. Acknowledged as the mightiest group in the globe and rivalled only by The Warsaw Pact, notorious for a series of drunken performances during which many of their own members got beaten up, NATO's own act became increasingly bloated and unwieldy, with trillions of dollars spent on stage equipment that would never be used. Rumours began to circulate of money problems, arguments and even dark ceremonies involving millions of dollars being sacrificed to right-wing terrorists.

Despite this, when The Warsaw Pact eventually folded in the early 1990s, many of its members decided to combine their forces with NATO. Soon even France was welcomed back into the fold, its unique stylings a welcome addition to the line-up. It was not long before NATO was performing in venues it had never visited before, preaching a new message of peace and reconstruction – accompanied by lots of heavy metal bombing – in the former Yugoslavia and Afghanistan.

Facing an ever-heavier tour schedule, band relations became increasingly fractious, with America – backed by Britain – spending more and more of its time on ill-conceived concept project Bombing the Heck out of Iran and the even more ludicrous Invading Iraq. Differences became ever stronger and when, in 2006, America and Britain called for members to get together for a rooftop concert in Afghanistan, only two Latvians turned up.

NATO was buried at David St Hubbins's Church of the Relic of the Past. The ceremony was led by Britain and America, though followed by almost nobody. The reading was from the book of St John the Betjeman (New Revised Version) 'Come friendly bombs and fall wherever the President wants'.

The Nuclear Non-Proliferation Treaty
1968–2006

The Nuclear Non-Proliferation Treaty was reduced to a pile of radioactive dust today in a moving ceremony held in North Korea, having passed away suddenly this morning in an explosion brighter than the sun and louder even than the noise George Bush made when he saw his latest poll ratings. The ceremony, whose charming centrepiece was the exploding of a nuclear weapon, was carried out underground, a move necessitated by the fact that the North Korean government had already laid waste to most of the country's surface and quite a few of its people.

Born on 1 July 1968, The Treaty decreed that only the five permanent members of the United Nations Security Council – the US, Russia, China, Britain and France – would be permitted to possess nuclear weapons. Its astonishing success during its lifetime can be seen from the fact that no other state ever came into possession of such devastating weapons, unless you count India, Israel, Pakistan, any country ever visited by a disgruntled former Soviet nuclear scientist in desperate need of cash to pay off his gambling debts, or Fox News. Many experts believe The Treaty was in poor health for most of its short life, though it soldiered on manfully, ignoring persistent nagging problems such as the many countries who refused to sign up to join it despite a suspicious tendency to glow in the dark and produce a surprising number of three-eyed fish.

The funeral was marred by heckling from representatives of the US who condemned the funeral as 'a provocative act', while senior Republicans proposed reducing global stockpiles of nuclear weapons by launching a pre-emptive strike on Iran or, failing that, on Canada, for its unilateral production of uranium-enriched Celine Dion albums and its hostile mispronunciation of 'aboot'. Despite this, few allowed their enjoyment of proceedings to be dimmed, with several nuclear bunker salesmen seen rubbing their hands with glee and dancing jigs with shotgun manufacturers and End Timers getting ready for Armageddon.

The Nuclear Non-Proliferation Treaty is survived by irradiated cockroaches and wheelchair-bound Germanic scientists with a weird resemblance to Peter Sellers crying out, *'Mein Fuhrer!'*

The Republicans' Control of the House of Representatives

1994–2006

The White House and friends of President Bush's administration were in mourning today following the death of The Republicans' Control of the House of Representatives, which passed away after contracting a long and destructive illness during an ill-advised foreign business trip to Iraq.

The Republicans' Control was born in 1994, to the surprise of many, no one more so than President Bill Clinton, who was immediately forced to deny he was the father.

Under the guiding hand of Speaker Newt Gingrich, The Republicans' Control quickly found its feet and began bullying Democrat initiatives in the House, picking on the poor and the huddled masses and, in 2000, winning the White House for its sidekick, George W. Bush.

After 9/11, The Republicans' Control began its work in earnest with the introduction of the Patriot Act, which required all US citizens to check their civil liberties at the door. Although 2001 was a busy year, The Republicans' Control did find time for an overseas vacation in Afghanistan, where it hoped to be reunited with an old family friend, Osama bin Laden.

However, a never-ending series of political and financial scandals left The Republicans' Control weakened and gasping for breath and President Bush's approval ratings dropped to a dangerous level. Desperate neoconservatives began an infusion of billions of dollars in a futile bid to stop the decline, sadly to no avail, as Americans began to question The Republicans' Control's determination to remain in the disputed region of the White House despite not having a clear exit programme.

Sadly, a last-minute attempt at foot-in-mouth resuscitation by America's leading stand-up comedian, John Kerry, failed to revive its health and The Republicans' Control was read the last rites, as it made its peace with God and other prominent backers of the party. The Republicans' Control suffered a series of fatal attacks, losing control of South Baghdad, North Baghdad, East and West Baghdad and most of Iraq, while Oliver North, the Republican challenger for the southern state of Nicaragua, lost again to Daniel Ortega.

The Republicans' Control of the House of Representatives will be buried somewhere in the wee small hours of Fox News bulletins.

Science and

Technology

The Compilation Tape

*c.*1970s–2007

The Compilation Tape, that marvel of magnetic sound recording that allowed a generation of men to woo women with a collection of their favourite tracks – and a generation of women to listen for two minutes before recording Abba's Greatest Hits over the lovingly-crafted tribute – has passed away following electrical retailer Currys' decision to stop selling audio cassettes.

Though the audio cassette was born in the early 1960s, it wasn't until the 1970s that the male of the species hit upon the romantic potential of ham-fistedly hitting 'Play' and 'Record' just after Peter Powell stopped his intro and, psychically, hitting 'Stop' before he started talking again – a technique which if completed successfully could result in a swoon-inducing 40-second version of 10cc's 'I'm Mandy, Fly Me'.

With the advent of separate cassette decks and turntables, The Compilation Tape found its popularity growing ever greater. Now men could spend hours, if not days, locked in the dank fug of their bedrooms, beavering away feverishly in order to demonstrate their encyclopaedic musical knowledge, cultural sophistication, emotional depth and desire to ~~get their end away with~~ prove their undying and noble love for the barmaid who had smiled at them… no really… whilst handing them a bag of pork scratchings with their pint of Double Diamond.

With the advent of younger, more exciting recording technologies – such as the minidisc, the rewritable CD and MP3 – that could do it longer, more frequently (and oh-so-much-more quickly…), The Compilation Tape suddenly found itself out-performed and, soon thereafter, cruelly spurned. Crushed by the knowledge that the wow and flutter wasn't the music of the inamorata's quickening pulse, but the mechanical failure of the cassette player as it chewed its way through the definitive live version of Bruce Springsteen's 'Hungry Heart', it slurred slowly to an end as The Tape became caught in the mechanism, crinkling its last.

The Compilation Tape will be consigned to the dusty cardboard box in the attic or, worse, cruelly dumped. The service will be conducted by the Right Reverend Nick Hornby and the congregation will sing along with Dave's 'I Love You, Cheryl 1987' C-90, wiping away a tear of joyous reminiscence to Human League's 'Love Action', sniggering into the hand-written liner notes at Englebert Humperdinck's 'Lesbian Seagull', guffawing uncontrollably to Salt 'n' Pepa's 'Push It' and thinking 'Ooh, that's a bit creepy' to The Police's 'Every Breath You Take (I'll Be Watching You)'.

It is survived by The CD Compilation, the iMix and the continuing failure of men to understand that if they spent some time with their significant others rather than locking themselves up with their MP3s they might stand half a chance of getting somewhere.

Digital Rights Management
1996–2007

Digital Rights Management (DRM) for music files – the software locks that prevent you playing iTunes music on your Sony Walkman, using your iPod to store tracks from Windows Media Player and makes it much more annoying to make ~~illegal~~ backup copies for personal use of your favourite tunes – has been declared dead following the decision by Apple and EMI to abandon the copyright protection system. Now, for an extra 20p, 'audiophiles' will be able to download the 'music' of Robbie Williams, Coldplay, Joss Stone and Lily Allen and make as many copies as they like for others, thus threatening to drown the globe in an unprecedented deluge of the musical equivalent of magnolia paint.

DRM was born in 1996, the youngest of a whole family of corporate killjoys including 'Home Taping is Killing Music', 'I Say, Making Copies of Wax Cylinders Just Isn't Cricket, You Know' and that bit at the beginning of old episodes of *Mission Impossible*, where Peter Graves only gets to listen to his tape once before it bursts into a puff of smoke.

Like most other music companies, Apple wholeheartedly embraced the use of DRM to prevent piracy, but the plan backfired when they found that once people had downloaded Robbie Williams, Coldplay, Joss Stone and Lily Allen, they didn't want to make endless copies of the tracks but instead found themselves overwhelmed by a desire to smash their brand new iPod into a thousand pieces before running down Chris Martin with his own Toyota Prius and beating him about the head with a branch hewn from one of his own carbon-offset forests.

Further blows to DRM came when it was realised that it had absolutely no effect on professional pirates who – unimpaired by their peg legs and hook-hands – always managed to break any form of copy-protection in less time than it takes Steve Jobs to pull on a black turtleneck, leaving only the humble consumer to suffer. And suffer they did, especially in 2005, when it was discovered that some Sony CDs were surreptitiously installing copyright protection on listeners' computers, thus interfering with their privacy and affecting the smooth running of Microsoft Windows, even more than Microsoft Windows itself affected the smooth running of Microsoft Windows.

Soon, music-lovers were clamouring for the right to download their favourite tracks to listen to as they pleased – whether on their computer, iPod, MP3 player, burnt to CD, cut to vinyl, taped onto an old C-90 found in their shed or banged out by that spare symphony orchestra they'd left in the attic. EMI relented, removed the software locks from its digital downloads and DRM was deleted for the last time.

DRM will be buried at the Jolly Pirate public house this weekend. The congregation will download Robbie Williams' 'Angels' for 99p... and then bury that as well. It is survived by Robbie Williams, Coldplay, Joss Stone and Lily Allen. This dodo will self-destruct in five seconds.

Gravity

*c.*13.7 Billion BC–AD 2007

Gravity (or, as its friends in the physics community knew it, 'Gravitational Force') has gone to join The Ether, Phlogiston and Victoria Beckham's Tan among the choir invisible of scientific no-noes, following the inauguration of the Grand Canyon Skywalk – a glass-bottomed horseshoe-shaped construction which allows visitors to stand in mid-air 4,000 feet above salivating coyotes, rattlesnakes and personal injury lawyers shouting, 'Jump!'

Gravity was born roughly 13.7 billion years ago with the formation of the universe. From the moment of its arrival, the heavy child set to work on its even heavier task of forming stars and planets, keeping celestial bodies in orbit and ensuring that when you place a cup on the coffee table it's still there five minutes later and the scalding coffee hasn't floated up and burnt the underside of your chin while you're reading the newspaper.

Despite this seemingly useful physical property, man longed to slip his earthly bonds and float free above the earth or, in Daedalus's case, let his son Icarus take out those new wax wings he'd invented on a test run, 'You know, just in case…'

It was as Isaac Newton prepared his lawsuit against Gravity after being brained by a Cox's Pippin that, he accidentally stumbled across the three gravitational laws that (quite literally) underpinned Gravity's lifelong purpose. Though the subsequent court case failed, Gravity's secret hold on Earth was fatally loosened from its fingers.

AS A DODO

Soon, man was clamouring to rise up, up and away in his beautiful balloon and dreaming of faster and higher trips into the blue. The Wright Brothers' early beach-hopping experiments inspired Wernher von Braun to design the rockets that ~~destroyed much of London during the final years of World War Two~~ allowed man to finally escape Earth's atmosphere and put Neil Armstrong, Buzz Aldrin et al. on the Moon.

Meanwhile, for ordinary earthlings not fortunate enough to make the grade as NASA graduates or have the necessary millions to join Stephen Hawking on the so-called 'Vomit Comet', the only chance of escaping Gravity was to take their lives in their hands on amusement park rollercoasters or a short-haul low-cost flight.

Inspired by the mid-air back-pedalling of Wile E. Coyote, construction began on the Grand Canyon Skywalk in 2004 – the ingenious addition of a glass walkway ensuring that visitors would not plummet earthwards, leaving a visitor-shaped hole in the canyon floor below... before being flattened by a loosened boulder... a falling grand piano... and an ACME anvil...

As Buzz Aldrin stepped out onto the Skywalk with the immortal words, 'It's one small step for man, one giant step for... Buzz Aldrin...! Yeah, that's right...! Buzz F★★kin' Aldrin...! In your face, Neil Armstrong!', Gravity was done for and let slip its grip on the world.

Gravity will not be buried but released directly into the heavens to drift slowly upwards into the wide, blue yonder – if it doesn't collide with a plethora of 747s, spy satellites or Professor Stephen Hawking.

Humanity's Sense of Superiority

*c.*2.5 Million BC–AD 2007

The death of Humanity's Sense of Superiority over its fellow creatures will come as a shock to all those who – while troubled by such daily cares as the grind of work, the quest for love or the renewed threats of both nuclear conflict and appearances by Noel Edmonds on TV – were able to console themselves with the knowledge that they were at least brighter than a chimp.

The Sense of Superiority's death comes following the discovery by researchers from the Leverhulme Centre for Human Evolutionary Studies in Cambridge that Senegalese chimpanzees band together to hunt using hand-crafted (or, rather, hand-and-tooth-crafted) spears – thus proving themselves to possess two of humanity's most highly prized assets: a) the ability to make use of tools and b) the ability to get their kicks by running around killing things.

Humanity's Sense of Superiority was born in around 2.5 million BC when early hominid *Australopithecus* first discovered how to make simple digging tools from polished stones, thus enabling her to dig further and faster than rivals without endangering her nails. This opened up new and exciting manicure possibilities as well as a diet of previously unreachable tubers, so paving the way for the potato to take over the diet of Western human beings two-and-a-half-billion years later.

The Sense of Superiority was to go from strength to strength when another human ancestor, *Homo erectus*, discovered how to make use of tools to create fire, either after watching the effects of a lightning strike on the arid African savannah in which he lived or as part of a complex scam involving taking out a million rocks' worth of fire insurance on his home tree. The use of fire immediately put the hominid one-up on all his fellow creatures, enabling him to bask in the glow of his Superiority, not to mention the embers of his former home and a brand new million-rock fortune.

Soon mankind was wandering across the whole globe, feeling smug as he set fire to things and made use of tools which steadily advanced from simple heated cooking stones, through bows and arrows all the way to such modern-day tools as the computer and the BBC weatherman who signs off with 'And that's your weather... for now'.

While Humanity's Sense of Superiority initially seemed to survive the potentially fatal discovery that fellow primates were also capable of making use of tools to assist them in achieving their goals, it fell into a steep decline when it realised that, rather than spending its time making computers and watching annoying weathermen, it could have spent the last two million years happily running around chasing things with sticks.

Humanity's Sense of Superiority will be cremated, just as soon as the chimps succeed in working out what to do with the matches. It is survived by Charlton Heston, a half-buried Statue of Liberty and a bunch of damned dirty apes.

The Incandescent Light Bulb

*c.*1870–2006

The whole of Britain will be plunged into darkness tonight following the unexpected death of The Incandescent Light Bulb, burnt out after almost 140 years of service.

Born in the latter part of the nineteenth century to at least twenty-five different inventors, all of whom claimed to have been on the scene at the time of its conception, The Incandescent Light Bulb was to brighten up evenings and nights across the globe for more than a century.

Ever eager to please, The Incandescent Light Bulb thrust itself into the world of entertainment. Soon it was adorning the dressing-room mirrors of West End stars and the fronts of the finest cinemas, not to mention adopting a fetching red hue in order to illumine the front windows of several Soho haunts favoured by MPs, judges, top celebrities and sad men incapable of forming a meaningful relationship. Within mere decades it had brought light to the most desolate and depressing places in Britain, including even parts of Blackpool, where 'The Illuminations' are ritually celebrated to this day by groups of pensioners high on Stone's Ginger Wine and hen parties high on alcopops.

In the flowering of The Bulb's success lay the seeds of its failure. As it expended ever more energy on banishing the darkness, The

Bulb found itself cast in the role of profligate planet-destroyer by concerned scientists and economists as well as politicians eager to be seen to do something about climate change without having to, as the case may be, a) talk to Gordon Brown about tax changes or b) give up jetting off on fact-finding missions and having swanky official cars driving behind them just out of camera shot on the daily cycle ride to work.

The tide of opinion turning against it, The Incandescent Light Bulb soon found itself under threat from lower-energy lighting alternatives, including compact fluorescent lamps and random acts of arson. Increasingly lonely and unloved, and forced to rely for what little popularity it could retain on the frequent retelling of ever-more-tired jokes about the number of persons required to change it, The Incandescent Light Bulb was eventually to pass away following a collision with The Stern Review on the Economics of Climate Change and Environment Minister David Milliband.

The Incandescent Light Bulb will be buried by new green taxes. The Bulb is survived by millions of TVs left on standby and the energy policy of the United States of America.

162

The Internal Combustion Engine

c.1879–2007

The Internal Combustion Engine has coughed and spluttered its last, suffering from terminal indigestion triggered by that dodgy litre of petrol it bought at a supermarket petrol station in the south of England this week.

The Internal Combustion Engine was born of doubtful parentage in the late nineteenth century, although Karl Benz laid claim to it with his patent for a four-stroke engine. It was a large and greedy baby requiring constant feeding with petrol-based snacks and spent its youth roaming the countryside frightening women, horses and the people of Norfolk. Indeed, it was considered so dangerous that, by law, a man was required to walk in front of it waving a red flag – sending terrified Edwardians into the nearest chemist for a reassuring tincture of laudanum.

In 1913, with Henry Ford mass-producing his infamous 'automobiles' built around The Engine, it was only a matter of months before millions were spending their last dimes on feeding the noisy, belching brat in pursuit of the American dream of life, liberty, happiness and bigger engines, bigger tyres and bigger overdrafts.

Around the world, sensible, horse-drawn members of society abandoned their quiet lives to become 'travelling salesmen' – willing to work harder and further away from home to feed their mechanical offspring and their need to cruise at 55 mph in the middle of the motorway regardless of the emptiness of the inside lane.

The Engine's constant demands for attention played a part in the decline of organised religion as supplicants worshipped at a new altar, preferring to spend their Sundays tinkering with their beloved Engines before going for a nice drive in the country – spending four hours stuck in a traffic jam on the A12, arguing with their partner about whether they really should have taken that last left and stopping for a relaxing cup of tea from a thermos on the hard shoulder of the M25.

With the price of petrol being driven up by decreased stability in oil-producing regions that, completely coincidentally, had recently been invaded by forces looking to develop peace, stability and new oil exploitation opportunities, many owners were driven (literally) to find cheaper fuel for their voracious Engines and started frequenting supermarket petrol station forecourts, looking for a cheap gallon of own-brand fuel to keep the over-sized wheels of their 4x4s turning and possibly a microwaveable burger for themselves. The ill-effects of a lifetime of reckless combustion combined with a last meal of contaminated petrol brought about The Internal Combustion Engine's inevitable end as, bloated, unwieldy and starved of oxygen, it had one final seizure and rolled to a silent halt by the side of the road, out of sight even of a Little Chef.

The Internal Combustion Engine will be placed in an unleaded casket inside a Rover Maestro before being scrapped at St Clarkson's Turbo-Charged Church of the Petrol-Head. It is survived by the bicycle, Shank's pony, Virgin Trains and irreversible climate change.

The Planet Pluto
1930–2006

The Planet Pluto has passed away, aged 76, after being officially downgraded to a mere dwarf planet by the International Astronomical Union.

Pluto, long believed to be the ninth true planet of the solar system, was discovered in 1930 at the Lowell observatory in Flagstaff, Arizona by one Walt Disney, who caused consternation among the whole astronomical community when he claimed the planet was actually a small, brown dog that orbited Mickey Mouse. Following Mr Disney's removal to a well-known rest home for the insane ('Hollywood'), Pluto was finally identified as a small planet circling the sun at the very edge of the solar system. Observations over the next 70 years revealed it to be a small and desolate location almost wholly lacking in atmosphere, leading many to confuse it with Leicester.

During it's 76 years in the solar system, Pluto was an enthusiastic – some might say over-enthusiastic – planet, trying to draw attention to itself with its jauntily slanted orbit, attempts to sneak up on the sun while Neptune's back was turned and its party trick of turning its somewhat sparse atmosphere into ice every time it approached the solar system's fringes. As the years went by, Pluto also began to hang out with other, less reputable astronomical bodies including Ceres and the leather-bookmark-skirted Xena. Eventually, the other planets decided they had no alternative but to pull the plug on their brash companion, particularly after its failure to make it either as a caramel-and-nougat-based chocolate bar or gain an entry into Gustav Holst's *The Planets* suite.

The Planet Pluto was quietly buried on Thursday along with its moons Charon, Nix and Hydra, in a moving ceremony attended by the remaining members of the solar system, marred only when Neptune and Mercury kept calling out Uranus's name and giggling.

The Slow Train

1825–2007

The Slow Train – the backbone of Britain's
'integrated transport system' for nearly
two hundred years – has died of shame
following the news that a French TGV
(Train à Grand Vitesse – one of those French
phrases which cannot be exactly translated into
English but means something like 'non-British train' or
'untortoiselike means of locomotion that will not break down
five miles out of Paddington') has broken the world land speed
record after travelling at 356 mph between Paris and Strasbourg
(despite attempts to prevent the record by three men wearing
stripey jumpers, berets, false moustaches and strings of onions,
who were later arrested for impersonating French train drivers
and named as Jeremy le Clarkfils, James Mais-Oui et Ricard
Hammond-Legume).

The Slow Train was born in 1825 – the offspring of Richard
Trevithick's steam locomotive (which was so slow it was
practically stationary) and the desire to transport goods and
passengers between points A and B faster than a team of sloths
on Diazepam. George Stephenson's optimistically-named Rocket
travelled between Stockton and Darlington at speeds of up to 29
mph, although when encumbered with passengers and goods it
could only manage a measly 12 mph… if moving downhill and
with a following wind.

For nearly two centuries, The Slow Train became a feature of everyday British life, much-loved by comedians... and much-hated by anyone who had to make a connection at Crewe by midday, travel between Cardiff and Swansea in under three weeks or failed to appreciate the delights of having their nose pressed into a stranger's armpit whilst the train stopped inexplicably between stations for longer than even Tantalus had to endure.

With the privatisation of British Rail in the mid-1990s, The Slow Train reached its finest hour (which occurred at least forty-five minutes later than the time printed on the timetable), as first the Conservatives and then Labour ensured that passengers would never again have to experience the horror of travelling faster than a nun on a bicycle or suffer the shock of arriving at their destination on time.

With the news that the French TGV had broken the world speed record for a train on rails – moving along the line faster than Keith Richards snorting his father's ashes – the last Slow Train in Britain (last Tuesday's 17.42 from Guildford to Woking, expected to arrive a week on Thursday) pulled into a siding and broke down for the last time.

The Slow Train will be buried at the John Major Church of the Privatised Railway. This service has been delayed and mourners are advised to use other forms of transport to reach their final destination.

The Slow Train is survived by The Stationary Train, The Train Withdrawn From Service and The Train Now Standing at Platform Nine Isn't a Train – It's a Virgin Express.

Smart-1

2003–2006

Smart-1, the European Space Agency's lunar probe, ended its life this morning by crashing into the Lake of Excellence on the Moon, having rejected the Bay of Averageness and Pond of Pillinger as its last resting place. Friends at ESA claim the probe had always wanted to die in this fashion, smashed into a million pieces on the barren surface of another world, which was lucky given that so many of ESA's projects end that way.

The washing-machine shaped probe was launched on 27 September 2003 and took nearly three years to reach the Moon, leading many to speculate it was designed by the combined efforts of contestants on *The Apprentice* and *Dragons' Den* and launched by Richard Branson.

Propelled by a solar-powered ion thruster instead of a chemical combustion engine, Smart-1 made its way to the moon after a complex series of spiral orbits, enabling the tiny but constant thrust from its engine to accelerate it to enormous speed while also avoiding the London congestion charge. Once in orbit round the Moon, the probe took thousands of photographs, mapping the lunar surface and conducting an exhaustive survey of its mineral composition for the benefit of science, mankind and Exxon, BP and Shell.

As well as studying the Moon, Smart-1 also spent the last 16 months of its short life testing innovative technologies of microscopic size, giving hope that it will one day be possible to crash Prince, Paul Daniels or Tom Cruise on the Moon.

The probe smashed into the surface of the Moon at 05.42 GMT, 3 September, at 5,000 mph, throwing up a dust cloud visible from the Earth and scattering its broken remains over a 10 m crater which has already been named the Lake of Discarded Rubbish, and caused lunar officials to issue ESA with an ASBO for fly-tipping.

Smart-1 is survived by NASA's Orion shuttle project, which plans to fulfil President George W. Bush's $230 billion pledge to put a man on the Moon by 2020. Sadly there is as yet no news as to whether the man in question will be George Bush himself.

The VHS Tape
1976–2007

The VHS Tape has unspooled for the last time, its glossy surface ripped from its plasticky exterior by economists at the Office of National Statistics, who have extracted it from the shopping basket of goods and services used to judge the rate of inflation and thrown it into the bin alongside brie, vegetable oil and sprouts.

The Video Home System, known to millions simply as 'the VHS' or (every time it unaccountably failed to record the whole of one's favourite programme) 'that bloody thing', was born in 1976. Even as it emerged from the womb of the JVC corporation it was to find rival mother Sony standing over it, pillow in hand, as it prepared to smother the child in favour of its own offspring, Betamax. Fortunately, the errant Japanese corporation was dragged away to a quiet room and, despite its inferior picture, VHS was ultimately to triumph over its rival after impressing the public with the size of its recording capacity. Thus began VHS's popularity as millions marvelled at their ability to record TV programmes while they were out… and then leave them unwatched until they were taped over a few days later.

The VHS Tape was to prove a major stepping stone in the life of many a child. Not only did it give the average five-year-old their first opportunity to triumph over their parents by being able to tape hour after hour of *Battle of the Planets* while the adults could only manage a recording that ended halfway through *Bullseye*, it also gave millions of impressionable adolescents the chance to broaden their cultural education by watching fifth generation pirate copies of *Driller Killer*.

With the birth of its younger sibling, The VHS Camera, The VHS Tape enjoyed amazing commercial success enabling people to video their own weddings and birthday parties – and then send the oh-so-hilarious results to Jeremy Beadle's *You've Been Framed* – and later allowing unknown micro-personalities such as Abi Titmuss to become very-well-known micro-personalities when recordings of their most intimate moments somehow found their way to the desks of every newspaper and PR agency.

It was the introduction of digital technology which saw The VHS Tape facing its final rewind. Its binary relative, The DVD, stole the show and viewers' affections by being able to provide movies with a sharper picture, surround sound and a commentary from the director's chauffeur's uncle's sister at the push of a button.

The VHS Tape deteriorated rapidly – stretching and distorting the picture and losing its sound quality in a gale of white noise – at which point the ONS consultants agreed that it no longer had a sustainable quality of life and, for the last time, gently untangled it from the playback heads and replaced it in its tired and worn-out cardboard sleeve.

The VHS Tape will be buried at car boot sales and charity shops across the country. It is survived by The DVD-RW, The Hard-Disk Recorder and accidentally deleting that episode of *The Persuaders!* on ITV4 you really wanted to watch.

172

YouTube
2005–2006

As a Dodo can today confirm reports that the 18-month-old video-sharing website YouTube has died after being swallowed up by a giant Google whale while paddling in lawyer-infested waters.

Born in February 2005, from the outset YouTube had a simple mission: to carry video communications from person to person across the waters of the worldwide web, allowing anyone anywhere in the world to share a little piece of their lives with others by posting their videos on the Internet. Few could have predicted how successful YouTube would be in its mission, while even fewer could have predicted that the bits of their lives people wanted to share were bad kung fu demonstrations, dodgy light-saber work-outs and lip-syncing demonstrations that would shame Milli Vanilli. Even more shocking was the fact that so many people's home videos bore an eerie (some would say exact) resemblance to old TV episodes and the latest music videos.

It was as the young Internet company was plunging blithely through the notorious sea of Digital Rights Management, Copyright and Trademark Infringements that, laden down with episodes of *Lost* and Madonna videos, it found itself surrounded by a school of great white media lawyers, eager for the scent of huge litigation dollars. With its attempts to struggle on hampered by several rare episodes of *The Six Million Dollar Man* and *Knight Rider*, it seemed certain that YouTube would soon be devoured by the vile creatures but fortunately it was able to swim to what appeared to be a nearby island while the lawyers argued over fee structures. Sadly, however, it appears that the island was in fact merely a killer Google whale. YouTube was swallowed whole.

YouTube was buried in the early hours of this morning, the officiant being a 72-year-old Japanese gentleman who lip-synced to Green Day's 'American Idiot' whilst wearing a Darth Maul costume. It is survived by a vast amount of litigation.

Society

The Bullingdon Club
c.Mid-nineteenth Century–2007

Waiting staff, pub landlords and other inhabitants of the city of Oxford are today breathing sighs of relief and downgrading their insurance policies, following news that The Bullingdon Club, Oxford University's most notoriously irresponsible 'dining club', must surely pass away after calls by its most celebrated member, Conservative Leader David Cameron, for a new 'responsible society'.

Born in the mid-nineteenth century (the details are, like so many members of the society, a little hazy) The Bullingdon Club was a late flowering of Regency irresponsibility in a more sober Victorian age. Though originally conceived as a sporting society, before its first year was out the club was already establishing for itself a reputation for drunkenness and debauchery previously only held by the Hellfire Club and now rivalled only by Premiership footballers and British under-30s on their summer holidays. It is understood that it is in order to distinguish themselves from the last two groups that The Club's members insist on wearing an eccentric uniform of blue tailcoats (though, sadly for The Club, this has led to many claims that former boxer and present-day oddball Chris Eubank is an honorary life member).

So irresponsible was The Club that, to this day, those invited to join are welcomed by having their rooms trashed (something which, admittedly, many students are capable of achieving without the aid of some chinless types in dinner dress) and then

176

required to book a private room at a local establishment where The Club's members can drink themselves into near insensibility before reducing the room to a state where it would look far from out of place in central Baghdad.

Down the years The Club's reputation grew. Lampooned by Evelyn Waugh as the Bollinger Club and attracting such (usually only briefly) upright members of society as bad artist and zookeeper Lord Bath, fraudster and thug Darius Guppy, gleefully caddish former minister Alan Clark and er, David Dimbleby, The Club spent its time in glorious irresponsibility, carrying out activities which lead lesser mortals to criminal charges and Club members to throw large amounts of daddy's money at the victims.

With members such as Shadow Chancellor George Osborne, Shadow Minister for Higher Education Boris Johnson and Mr Cameron himself all poised to take power, a future of untrammelled irresponsibility seemed assured. Who could have predicted that one of The Club's own offspring would forsake his vows and turn against it, using a speech to the Royal Society of Arts and an article in *The Guardian* to espouse the virtues of social responsibility and condemn those who cause wreck and ruin in their failure to offer others the respect that they deserve?

The Bullingdon Club will be buried at a secret dining event at St Alan Clark's Church of the Extended Wine Tasting. The vicar will read from the book of 'Dear Lord You Can't Really Be Doing That in the Font Can You? Oh, Here's £500 For the Church Roof, You Say? Just Carry On'. The church itself will be condemned as structurally unsound tomorrow.

Childhood

*c.*Mid-nineteenth Century–2007

The death of Childhood, confirmed by the publication of the government's new curriculum for the under-fives, cannot truly be counted as unexpected. Under increasing pressure from the joint effects of a society bent on buying girls under ten clothing bearing the *Playboy* magazine logo (whilst threatening to lynch everyone from paedophiles to paediatricians) and a government bent on cramming the maximum number of exams into the life of everyone under 25, the only cause for wonder is, perhaps, that it managed to survive so long.

While children have existed since time immemorial, Childhood was only born during Queen Victoria's reign, when people realised that children were not merely handily chimney-sized mini-adults but cherubic innocents, closer to the angels than the adults about them and ideal for being pictured on the cover of any chocolate box.

Freed from the close confines of assorted chimneys, coal mines and machine works, Childhood became a time of innocence and play, when the young could cherish the joys of tripping merrily through a meadow, blowing soap bubbles and fashioning daisy chains, or the even greater joys of scrumping apples, burning their dad's shed to the ground and making their parents' lives as miserable as possible.

Soon Childhood became so popular that many of those over retirement age (particularly senior judges) decided to indulge in it a second time. As the decades passed, more people began to realise that Childhood really was the best time of their lives. Increasingly, people well into their twenties, thirties and forties decided to cling onto Childhood (not to mention the childish things that went with it, such as Xbox 360s, doll collections and the belief that the *Harry Potter* books have some literary value).

It soon became clear that there was not enough Childhood to go around. Parents – urged on by a society eager to turn anyone capable of holding a coin into a consumer and a media eager to push pictures of semi-naked women at tweenies – rushed to thrust adulthood upon their offspring just as soon as they could find an ear-piercing salon willing to carry out its work *in utero*.

Alerted to the shortage of Childhood, the government, over the years from 1997, worked steadily to cut it down, loading everyone under 20 with so many standard assessment tests, GCSE exams, GNVQ exams, AS-level exams, A-level exams et al. that the only way that anyone could find time to trip merrily was to drop some acid on the way to the exam hall.

It was the government's curriculum for the under-fives – a curriculum that will test them on everything from their ability to count their toes to their capacity to programme a computer – that proved Childhood's end, crowding out the last period of time in a child's life not already filled with examinations. Starved of time, freedom and love, Childhood finally toddled into the night.

Childhood will be buried at St Herod's Church. The reading will be the first four words of Mark 10:14, 'Suffer the little children'.

The Christmas Club

0–2006

The Christmas Club has been found dead at its home in Farepak. Police believe it had disturbed burglars who may have made off with a Christmas hamper worth up to £40 million. They have warned members of the public not to approach the thieves or their associates, who may be posing as bankers, city gents and incompetent regulators.

The Christmas Club was conceived in the year 0 when a young, impoverished woman from Judea began saving the Almighty's seed in the nine months before 25 December. Fortunately, her husband's ire at being cuckolded by his wife and having to spend the festive season in a barn, was somewhat mollified by gifts of gold, frankincense and myrrh.

The Christmas Club quickly bloomed, enabling peasants throughout the ages to put aside a groat a week and enjoy a magical Yuletide – unless their family had been killed by the plague, killed by invading Anglo-Saxon or Viking or Norman hordes, killed by the King's men for gathering winter fu-el in the forest, or their family had been sold into slavery in order to make the weekly payments on The Christmas Club.

But it was with the introduction of the modern Christmas as we know it by Prince Albert (famous for stapling his Christmas cracker to his baubles) that The Christmas Club became popular throughout the great Victorian slums, workhouses, and poorhouses that made Britain the greatest country in the world.

Fattened by the increasing aspirational pressure applied by Our Lord Santa in the glittery advertisements shown from as early as late October on 72-inch flat screen tellies (available from all good electrical outlets), The Christmas Club became as bloated as one of its turkey-style Christmas roasts. In this state it inevitably attracted the interest of the murkier elements of the corporate world, an interest which was to lead to The Club's demise.

The Christmas Club was buried in an over-priced hamper at St Scrooge's Church. The congregation sang Slade's 'Merry Xmas Everybody'. The service was attended by friends and family including The National Lottery, National Insurance and Pension Schemes. The Christmas Club is survived by the Halifax, numerous other high street banks and a vast mountain of Christmas debt.

The Grammar School

1944–2007

Hundreds of middle-class parents are today tearing up their eleven-plus practice papers and lamenting the thousands they forked out for extra tuition in a desperate attempt to get their Nintendo DS-addicted Julian and Poppy through the eleven-plus examination, following the announcement by Conservative education spokesman David Willetts that The Grammar School has failed its final test and been condemned to The Great Secondary Modern in the Sky.

Though it could trace its origins back to Anglo-Saxon colleges of Latin grammar, the modern Grammar School was only born in 1944, following the passing of the Butler Education Act, which offered the children of domestic servants the chance not to follow in their fathers' footsteps.

In its early years The Grammar School was a popular child, with friends across the political spectrum. Alongside its brothers, The Technical College and The Secondary Modern, it promised to sweep away class divisions, granting a proper education to all and offering a real chance of advancement to any child. All this was to be achieved by the 'eleven-plus' examination, under which every child was categorised at the age of 11 according to their ability to say at what time the 11.32 from St Pancras will be derailed by the 12.27 from Nottingham if both were travelling at 120 mph.

The Grammar School had barely entered its teens when questions began to be raised about its fitness, as it became apparent that large proportions of the pupils at Grammar School (usually referred to by their parents as 'the clever ones') were middle class, while many of those at the other schools (usually referred to by the parents of the children at Grammar School as 'the thickies') were working class. Despite this, The Grammar School's fond parents in Westminster continued to dote upon it even to the extent of lavishing money on it at its siblings' expense.

Though The Grammar now found itself supplanted in many parts of Britain by a new and frightening rival, The Comprehensive, it still had many powerful friends and so struggled on. For decades it was able to rely on the support of the Conservative Party and thousands of parents eager to see Toby and Pippa do better than those children on the council estate they met at primary school, while at the same time being reluctant to splash out thousands on public school fees. Yet all seemed doomed when the Labour Party swept to power in 1997 and Education Secretary David Blunkett pledged to end all selection and break down class barriers – a goal he bizarrely attempted to achieve by mingling with the upper classes at parties held by *The Spectator*.

Even at this darkest hour, The Grammar School persevered, quietly whispering to senior members of the Labour Party how badly its death would play in the *Daily Mail* and how well the children of those very same party members might do if they got to go to a nice selective school rather than the local 'bog-standard' Comprehensive.

Yet how often the best laid plans gang agley. The Grammar School had sown the seeds of its own destruction. Even as the government reneged on its promises to end selection, so it created a new rival for The Grammar: The Academy. Young and fresh, The Academy was unhindered by The Grammar's historical baggage. It was backed by rich and powerful businessmen, eager to ~~indoctrinate the young~~ give something back to the community. It was able to select its pupils in more under-the-counter ways, seeking 'aptitude' where The Grammar had clung to 'IQ', and even interviewed pupils to check their suitability where The Grammar had been increasingly forced to stick to the arid results of an exam. It was little surprise when The Academy won even the heart of the Conservative Party and, increasingly unloved and ever more confused, The Grammar School sang the school song (in Latin) no more.

The Grammar School will be buried at St Cameron's Church of the Apostasy. The Reverend David Willetts will preside. The hymn will be the number that completes the sequence 12, 12, 13, 15, 18.

The Grammar School is survived by The Academy, The Faith School, The Public School, The Trust School and, just barely, by The Comprehensive School.

The London Stock Exchange
1698–2006

Trust fund managers, brokers and merchant bankers across Britain momentarily turned their heads from their screens/clients/vast piles of money this morning, following the news of the death of The London Stock Exchange (LSE), which drowned in the Thames last night after dining with a group of well-connected major investment banks.

The LSE was born in 1698 when one John Castaing, fired up by vast amounts of java, first pinned up a list of stock and commodity prices on the walls of Jonathan's Coffee House in London's Change Alley, with the aim of parting as many suckers as possible from their cash.

With its twin mottoes 'My word is my bond' and 'Your money is my money... and currently invested in an offshore intermediate revolving forex facility', The LSE was soon bestriding the financial world like the proverbial colossus, with those beneath it compelled to lift their gazes and contemplate the vast size and extreme goldenness of its twin fiscal spheres.

In the following years The LSE, red in tooth and braces, would become one of the world's most powerful financial forces, leading investors through South Sea Bubbles and Railway Mania to penury, while leading itself to vaster and vaster piles of money. By the early part of this century, those vast piles of money began to attract an increasing number of

185

suitors. Gossip columnists noted that the ageing LSE was seen out with a different partner each night, showing its commodities off to Deutsche Börse one evening, then flashing its sparkling derivatives at NASDAQ the next.

Such behaviour could not go unnoticed. Major investment banks which had long been associates of The LSE began to feel that their old friend, for whom they had done so much, was spending too much time gadding about and building up money piles and not enough showing them the respect they deserved. Attempts at reconciliation – including gifts of horses' heads – were made, the last of them occurring when the banks invited The LSE to dine with them. It appears that, clearly fearful of the current inclement weather, The LSE made the tragic mistake of wearing a concrete overcoat for its walk back from the restaurant along the Embankment, leading to inevitable tragedy when a pat on the back from several of its bank pals caused it to fall into the river, where it drowned. The banks made repeated attempts to rescue The LSE by dropping heavy metal chains on it and shooting it but all to no avail.

The London Stock Exchange will be buried at St Mammon's Church. Well-wishers are asked to send cash. The LSE will be survived by the major investment banks, their brand new European share market and vast piles of money.

Low Inflation
1992–2007

Bank managers and building society heads were today united in sadness at the death of Low Inflation, a sadness which they chose to express by immediately cancelling all their low-rate, fixed-interest mortgage offers and preparing to issue foreclosure notices against any debtor who considered looking at them in an even slightly needy way.

Low Inflation was born in the UK in 1992, the product of Chancellor of the Exchequer Norman Lamont's decision to jilt the European Exchange Rate Mechanism in favour of a brief bathtub liaison with a sexy floating pound. So disturbing was this event – not to mention the image of Norman Lamont in a bath inextricably associated with it – that it will forever be known as Black Wednesday. It was in this dark period that Low Inflation first saw the light of day in the British economy, perhaps due to the fact that at the time there was precious little British economy left to inflate.

Over the following years, Low Inflation was to dominate the British economic scene, ushering in a time of prosperity, rapidly rising house prices and spending like there was no tomorrow on essential 1990s items like Magic Eye posters, PlayStation consoles and Robson and Jerome tapes. So popular was Low Inflation that in 1997 new Chancellor Gordon Brown placed it at the centre of his policies, right alongside blaming the Conservative Party for anything that went wrong and wishing Tony Blair was dead. This ushered in a period of yet more prosperity, even more rapidly rising house prices and spending like there wasn't even much of today left on essential late-twentieth century items like *Harry Potter* books, interactive CDs and DVD players.

Such a golden age could not last. By the early noughties the British economy was beginning to show a fatal addiction to ever more expensive energy sources and an unfortunate tendency to drop bombs on the places that provided them. This, combined with rapidly rising house prices and spending like the world was about to end on essentials like ultra-slim jeans, Arctic Monkeys MP3s and giant flat-screen tellies, was ultimately to lead to Low Inflation's death.

Low Inflation will be buried under a mountain of overextended credit cards and unsecured debt. It is survived by some very rich energy company officials and a lot of people wondering if an LCD TV the size of a football pitch was really an essential purchase.

Man's Best Friend

*c.*12,000 BC–AD 2007

Man's Best Friend has rolled over and played dead for the last time following the announcement that Eli Lilly, the manufacturer of Prozac, has produced Reconcile – a chewable, beefy-flavoured selective serotonin re-uptake inhibitor for dogs – freeing the canine world from the centuries of depression that fuelled its desperate need to buddy up to man.

Man's Best Friend, *Canis lupus familiaris*, is descended from wolves, those deeply unhappy creatures that were forced to sublimate their terrible inner turmoil and lack of self-confidence into growling, sheep-savaging and appearances in horror movies until they realised that by hanging around on the fringes of human settlements and howling forlornly at the moon they might get mankind to take pity and domesticate them.

Soon Man's Best Friend was earning his keep by fetching and carrying Stone Age slippers (not easy for a Chihuahua), begging oh-so-cutely for scraps of food at the table and enthusiastically shagging the leg of any passing visitor, all in an attempt to disguise the terrible futility and endless ennui of a dog's life.

Over the long, lonely millennia Man's Best Friend sank into a deep pit of despair, exacerbated by its maintenance of a furry, upbeat facade as it chased sticks, wagged its tail and pretended it enjoyed being done up like a dog's dinner and paraded in front of its peers at humiliating dog shows around the globe.

Deeply frustrated at its failure to communicate its growing depression to mankind, it spent increasing hours chewing the furniture, barking 'And what time do you call this?' at the postman and sleeping in its basket – where its disturbing dreams clouded by thoughts of self-harm and the pointlessness of existence were, tragically, misinterpreted by its owners, who simply cooed, 'Aw… He's dreaming about cats…!'

Attempts by Man's Best Friend to deal maturely with his 'black dog' were cruelly thwarted when therapists refused to counsel him – sharply ordering the four-pawed patient to get off the couch. That a turning point had been reached became clear last year, with claims that several hundred show dogs – unable to cope with the burden of being in the public spotlight as they fought to mask their crushing loneliness – threatened a mass suicide at Crufts.

The release of Reconcile onto the market has sent a (high-pitched and inaudible) signal to the doggie world that its unhappy dependency on man is over. Dogs in their millions have besieged their vets begging (cutely) for a prescription of the canine happy pill that puts the spring back in their step and the smile back in their bark… Thus it is that Man's Best Friend has ceased to be a poodle.

Man's Best Friend will be wrapped in his favourite blanket and buried at the end of the garden next to that tree he almost killed by urinating on it copiously every day. It is survived by Man's New Best Friend who really, *really* does love you…! Yes he does…! *Yes* he does…!

NHS Dentistry

1948–2007

The snaggle-toothed inhabitants of Britain were
lining up in the streets outside dentists' surgeries
this morning, following the news that NHS
Dentistry has passed away, its jaws clamped shut and
its cries of protest muffled, after the publication
of a report revealing that two million patients
still don't have access to a dentist under the
National Health Service.

NHS Dentistry was born in 1948,
the offspring of the post-war Labour
government's dream of offering free
dentistry to all and their nightmare of
millions of ill-shaped British teeth chomping
down on their chip-butties for eternity.

For all the hope in which it was conceived, NHS Dentistry
quickly began to show signs of the split personality that would
afflict it throughout its life. Whilst purporting to be kind and
generous, it could at the same time be money-grabbing and
threatening. By the age of three it had already cast aside its practice
of treating all and sundry without charge and was demanding
payments of up to £1 with a hideously-squealing drill in one
hand and a hideously-squealing patient in the other. When simple
extortion proved insufficient to sate its lust for terror, NHS
Dentistry moved into the protection business, threatening its

victims with gnashers resembling Stonehenge and mouths full of gun-metal fillings unless they chose to hand over large portions of their cash and 'go private'.

With the service on the NHS growing poorer, patients were forced to fall into the arms of private dentistry or, like Her Majesty the Queen, resolve never to smile again. Soon the nation was divided into two classes: the gummy poor, their teeth whipped out in a sad attempt to evade the dental mafia, and the shiny-toothed rich, their molars bright but their wallets considerably lighter.

When, last year, the Tooth Fairy was murdered for 50p by a gang of freelance orthodontists, the game was finally up. Now almost wholly given over to private work, making free dental service scarcer than hens' – or, indeed, healthy British – teeth, NHS Dentistry had no choice but to apply the gas to itself.

NHS Dentistry will be buried at the Church of Laurence Olivier amidst much gnashing and wailing of patients' rotten teeth. It is survived by tying a string between the offending molar and a door-knob, ill-fitting dentures and endless American jokes about English teeth.

The Office Christmas Party

0–2006

The Office Christmas Party was found dead this morning in a bus shelter with a half-eaten kebab in its hand. It is believed to have died after over 2,000 years of drinking cheap wine and brightly-coloured cocktails, making multiple copies of its hairy hind-parts on the office photocopier and trying to get off with that middle manager in human resources finally took their toll.

The Office Christmas Party started its long and hedonistic life in Bethlehem when shepherds and wise men first got together to discuss office politics, have a likeness of their posterior fashioned in clay tablet and then tell that new angel that they're 'really lovely, no really…'

In its youth, The Office Christmas Party was extremely popular with under-serfs, and junior clerkes across the land. Much mead was consumed and illustrated manuscripts of apprentice monks' rear ends are now displayed in the finest museums across the globe.

But it was the dawn of the industrial age in the nineteenth century that saw The Office Christmas Party reach the zenith of its popularity. The Guild of Urchins, The Honourable Brethren of Chimney Sweeps and The Associated Pick-Pockets, amongst many corporations, looked forward to their annual works do, when they would drunkenly spread scurrilous rumours about their fellow urchins, chimney sweeps and pick-pockets and claim that Master Fotherington in the clerks' office had offered them a sight of his sweetmeats.

In its senior years, however, The Office Christmas Party became tiresome: drunkenly insisting staff exchange presents with people they managed to ignore for the rest of the year, clink glasses with the boss who promised them promotion then gave the job to that talentless idiot from accounts and play pin the tail on the sales chart, spin the stapler and post room knock.

Towards the end of its last night, The Office Christmas Party finally plucked up the courage to tell its new, 21-year-old manager exactly what it thought of him and his new plans for the department, and was immediately fired. Thinking it was just a joke, The Office Christmas Party continued to drink, finally staggering away from the building just before midnight, repeatedly muttering 'the bastards' under its breath.

The Office Christmas Party had asked to be cremated, but due to its massive intake of alcohol, senior management rejected this request on health and safety grounds. The Office Christmas Party will instead be buried on the third floor of the marketing department, in a broom cupboard.

The Office Christmas Party is survived by The New Year's Eve Party, The Birthday Party and The Wake for The Office Christmas Party which starts at lunchtime in the secretarial department, where it is expected that staff will drink cheap wine, brightly-coloured cocktails, make multiple copies of their hairy hind-parts on the office photocopier and try to get off with that middle manager in human resources.

The Veil

1300 BC–AD 2006

People across the globe will be shocked to learn today of the death of The Veil, which passed away this morning after a series of violent assaults by a selection of government politicians and the British press, led by Jack 'Do You Mind Undressing For Me, Love?' Straw.

Though always rather vague about its age, The Veil is believed to have been born some time prior to 1300 BC, when – according to ancient Assyrian gossip columnists – it spent most of its days enjoying face time with noblewomen and most of its nights hanging around with commoners and courtesans, a practice later to be taken up enthusiastically by British MPs and Premiership footballers.

After several centuries of such debauched behaviour, The Veil eventually decided to reform its ways following a serious of religious experiences. As many of these experiences involved deeply repressed religious men of senior years, The Veil took it upon itself to protect the world from the dreadful nubility of women, covering up their heads and faces lest they viciously inflame the hearts of deeply repressed religious men of senior years – who might happen to be, say, hanging around in alleyways or up ladders outside the women's houses desperate for a glimpse of nose or eyebrow.

Thanks to the sterling work of a range of deeply repressed religious men of senior years, within just a few centuries The Veil became common throughout the Middle East and Europe. Sadly its plans were to backfire, with its mere presence often serving merely to increase the erotic charge in any situation, something The Veil did little to help by going back to its old habits of appearing with erotic dancers and attractive young widows, as well as spending huge amounts of cash on really good eyeliner and mascara. Such mixed messages were ultimately to lead to tragedy, with a generation of teenage boys developing a permanent sexual fixation on Terry Jones after watching *Monty Python's Life of Brian*.

As the years passed and deeply repressed religious men of senior years began to lose their influence, The Veil started to fall from favour and from faces across Europe and many parts of the Middle East. Soon The Veil found itself increasingly ostracised. Lonely and unloved, it eventually became prey to attacks by unruly gangs, including 'The *Sun* Boys', 'The *Express* Crew' and 'The *Daily Mail* Fear Squad'. The incident that was to bring about its ultimate end came when it was grabbed by Jack Straw and used to bludgeon his way into the headlines.

The Veil leaves behind many deeply repressed religious men of senior years, hundreds of concerned makers of bridal wear and a lot of very confused liberals.

Sport

The 2012 British Olympic Spirit

2005–2007

The 2012 British Olympic Spirit was found dead this week in a partially built stadium on Hackney Marshes. Sources close to The Spirit say it had become increasingly worried after the estimated cost for the London Olympics more than trebled from £2.4 billion to £9.3 billion and have now risen so high that they have been selected for the pole vault squad.

The Spirit, the long-awaited offspring of Sebastian Coe and Tessa Jowell, was born amidst much fanfare and hoopla in July 2005 – although the fanfare and hoopla had less to do with the prospect of the nation being afforded an opportunity to display its sporting prowess to the rest of the globe and more to do with pipping the French bid at the post.

While other countries greet the prospect of hosting the Olympics as an occasion for national pride (not to mention a marvellous opportunity to rip off tourists), in ever-cheerful and optimistic Great Britain enthusiasm for the 2012 Olympic Games was, from the sound of the starting pistol, confined to construction firms and property developers gleefully shaking their heads, sucking in air and cackling, 'That's gonna cost you… We should be able to finish that by 2013, but we've got another job on down Wembley way…'.

With the Olympic ideal of the finest amateurs competing for nothing more than a crown of laurels and the approbation of their peers having long been cast aside in favour of the Olympic far-from-ideal of the worst professionals refusing even to compete in a charity sports day for less than £15,000, The Spirit – never strong – quickly began to wane. Rather than being galvanised into glorious action, across the land, Britain's potential medal winners of the future chose instead to slump back in their sofas, turn on *Richard & Judy* and wonder vaguely if Citius, Altius and Fortius were three of the Teenage Mutant Ninja Turtles.

Attempts to consolidate all its debts into one manageable debt failed to halt The Spirit's decline. Despite plans to raise capital by introducing sponsored events including the 400 m Financial Hurdles and the Snickers Marathon, and Mayor of London Ken Livingstone's plans to introduce a congestion charge for cyclists using the Olympic velodrome, the costs continued to spiral. The Spirit fell into a deeper and deeper depression before, tragically, taking its life, hanging itself with the ribbon of a genuine replica plastic Olympic gold medal bearing the legend 'I Love the 2012 Olympics' (retail price £29.99).

The 2012 British Olympic Spirit will be buried in a pauper's grave along with billions of taxpayers' cash as construction firms and property developers dance ecstatically in a New Orleans-style celebration of the dead. It is survived by Ken Livingstone, Tessa Jowell and the knowledge that if the French had won they'd have done the whole thing with a lot more class and a lot less whinging.

As a Dodo small print: the cost of your Olympics may go up as well as up, and your home may be at risk if you do not keep up council tax repayments.

Andrew 'Freddie' Flintoff's National Hero Status

1998–2007

Andrew 'Freddie' Flintoff's National Hero Status was born in 1998, the child of the precocious skills of a cheerful, six-foot-four cricketer from Lancashire and a press eager to build up any cricketing all-rounder as the new Ian Botham before condemning him to ignominy as the old Derek Pringle.

Even at such an early stage it was apparent to many that the man the nation would come to know as 'Freddie' possessed many of the skills of a great all-rounder. As a bowler he could inspire fear in batsmen, as a batsman he could inspire fear in bowlers and as a drinker he inspired awe in such greats as Jeffrey Bernard, Oliver Reed and George Best.

With such unique attributes at his command it was inevitable that Freddie would be granted National Hero Status. Over the years there were many heroic achievements: two wickets in the vital final over in a one day match against India in 2002 that led to a shirt-ripping display, centuries against South Africa and the West Indies along with five-wicket hauls in 2003–2004 with many more to come, not to mention still being able to fit through the cricket ground turnstiles in spite of a sustained onslaught of pints of bitter and tins of Fray Bentos.

Freddie's National Hero Status was to reach its apogee in 2005 when his feats of cricketing excellence during the Ashes Test series (and drinking excess after it) succeeded in winning him the admiration of a whole nation, not to mention an award from the National Brewers' Association for services to the industry. From such a peak, however, decline is inevitable.

In the following years, Flintoff found it hard to repeat the feats of his youth – whether on or off the field. With fame came responsibility and with the failure of Michael Vaughan's knee to survive anything beyond a shuffle out of the armchair to grab a newspaper came the responsibilities of the England captaincy. When England lost the Ashes to a resurgent Australia, Freddie's National Hero Status began to show signs of frailty.

It was during the Cricket World Cup in the Caribbean that the last innings was to be played. Over several hours in St Lucia's Rumours nightclub, Freddie – cheered on by his teammates – worked steadily, first grabbing a few singles before moving on to doubles, pints and chasers, with the prospect of an extra spicy goat curry on the way home and some serious runs later. It was not to be. Determined that his legend should live on, Freddie took the unfortunate decision to grab a pedalo and set out into Rodney Bay, where he capsized and his England vice-captaincy sank without trace.

Andrew 'Freddie' Flintoff's National Hero Status, along with the prospect of him ever captaining the England cricket team again – barring every other England-qualified human being capable of holding a bat being struck by lightning – was buried at sea. It is survived by David Gower's Tiger Moth, Mike Gatting's Reverse Sweeps and Geoffrey Boycott's Selfless Team-spiritedness.

Cricket Umpiring

1646–2006

The cricket world is mourning the sad demise of Cricket Umpiring following the self- immolation of Australian umpire Darrell Hair during the fourth test match between England and Pakistan at the Oval. In the early hours of the evening, Mr Hair decided to pour petrol over himself and international cricketing relations before setting light to it in protest over an alleged ball-tampering incident. Whose balls were allegedly tampered with, or why, we shall now never know, though friends of Cricket Umpiring have suggested that someone had attempted to 'grab Pakistan by the googlies'. Already the incident is being compared to the notorious 'Bodyform' Ashes series, in which England decided to target the brilliant Australian batsman Donald Bradman by bowling sanitary towels at him.

It was in 1646 that Cricket Umpiring first made its tentative appearance in the world, calling 'play' on a limited-overs match between two Kentish sides which sadly had to be abandoned almost immediately when bad light and the English Civil War stopped play. This was just the beginning of a troubled childhood: only two years later the whole game of cricket was banned by the new Puritan parliament, who regarded it as liable to induce ungodly merriment and impious consumption of cucumber sandwiches. Happily the game, and Umpiring along with it, returned to favour following the Restoration, when the newly-crowned King Charles II was informed that bowling a maiden over was a highly-prized feat in any cricket match. After this difficult youth, cricket and Umpiring soon grew to prominence on the world stage, bringing to the remotest parts of the Empire the deeply-held British values of decency, fair play and utter self-delusion, not to mention official incompetence.

Following its cremation, the last remains of Cricket Umpiring have been laid to rest in a small urn, whose ownership will be contested in a bi-annual contest between England and Pakistan, represented by ex-England captain Mike Gatting and the late Pakistani former umpire Shakoor Rana.

David Beckham's Spanish Career

2003–2007

Footballers will today sign a series of vastly over-remunerative sponsorship deals in memory of The Spanish Career of former England soccer captain David Robert Joseph Beckham, which has finally passed away after months of illness, bravely borne.

David Beckham's Spanish Career was born in 2003 to a barrow-load of money from Real Madrid and a blazing row with Sir Alex Ferguson. Within seconds of its birth it was hailed as a *galactico*, a Spanish term that translates into English as 'overpaid, big name footballer who will fail to assist Real's quest for a major trophy' – a role which David was to fulfil almost perfectly during the three-and-a-half years of his Spanish Career's life. From the outset he threw himself into his new role: despite many struggles and missteps he eventually came to grips with a complex language and, having finally mastered sufficient English to conduct an interview without the need to resort to signs, even went on to learn some simple Spanish words, including the phrases, 'How much will you pay me to do that?', 'Where is the mobile of Rebecca Loos?' and 'No, my wife's breasts are all her own, honest; the strange ridge at the top is due to a complex genetic condition'.

While matters off the field were going well, with regular appearances in celebrity gossip magazines and tabloids encouraging regular transfusions of

cash from major sponsors, matters on the pitch fared rather worse. Soon, The Career was showing signs of illness, with the young star that had burst onto the scene from the wing beginning to fizzle out – like so many over-swerved free kicks – meaninglessly in the middle of the pitch. It was not long before The Career was not even fit enough to make its regular cameo appearances from the bench and was instead transferred to the reserves where its final, sad moments could be kept from the media.

Despite such treatment, Beckham himself managed to keep his spirits to the last, even managing to joke with reporters gathered around The Career's deathbed that its end had nothing to do with Los Angeles Galaxy's £125 million offer and was 'all about the kids'. It was as the chorus of raucous laughter this quip engendered died down that The Career breathed its last.

A moving ceremony was held for David Beckham's Spanish Career during the summer, as a series of removal men transferred a vast amount of overpriced clothing and gold-plated furniture from Spain to Los Angeles. The Career is survived by *Hello!* magazine.

José Mourinho's Cool
1963–2007

The football world has abandoned its ridiculous pay demands, nightclub punch-ups and three-in-a-bed entertainments to mourn José Mourinho's Cool, that air of European style, tactical flair and self-confidence that has recently slipped away to be replaced by a grizzled figure in a tracksuit given to attacks on opposing teams and managers and claims that Mr Mourinho's pet Yorkshire terrier, Gullit, is a better finisher than Shevchenko.

José Mourinho's Cool was born in Portugal in 1963, holding its first press conference (in both Portuguese and English) acknowledging the skill of the midwife, protesting at the failure of the referee to book the attending doctor for an obvious slap and praising Mourinho's skill in choosing to be born.

After a childhood of dismissing inferior teachers with a snappy putdown and enlarging upon the magnificence of Mourinho's innate talent, The Cool saw its charge gain a degree in physical education without breaking a sweat, or even once shouting at other students that they'd have to do the class in their pants.

Too self-assured to chase a ball up and down the park for 90 minutes, José Mourinho's Cool contented itself with hanging around the stands delivering withering looks to opposition players and admiring itself lovingly in the changing room mirror at half-time. Word of The Cool began to spread, thanks chiefly to José Mourinho himself taking every opportunity to remind all and sundry of his superior intelligence, fashion sense and god-like footballing nous.

The Cool's self-confidence and magnetism drew players to Mourinho, as they sought a new style of coaching, a style The Cool was able to provide by offering tips on dead-ball situations, physical fitness advice and clear directions as to where to get a really first-class suit.

In 2004, José Mourinho's Cool announced itself to the hushed and adoring world of English football as 'The Special One', even more special than third-rate purveyors of ersatz, *Hello!* magazine-type cool like David Beckham. Over the next three years ~~Roman Abramovich's money~~ The Cool's know-how propelled its new club, Chelsea, to trophy after trophy. Yet signs of stress were already beginning to show, with The Cool melting in heated verbal assaults, attacking referees and fellow managers alike. With year after year passing and failure after failure to win the European Cup, questions began to be asked ... chiefly questions from Roman Abramovich like 'Oi, José! What is happen to my billions of roubles?' José Mourinho's Cool began to falter.

According to eye-witness reports, The Cool passed away when animal welfare officers called at José Mourinho's Belgravia home to put his Yorkshire terrier, Gullit, into quarantine, leaving the once-adored manager to shout 'No, please don't take my lickle-wickle Gullit away!' while stamping on his pipe with his Marks & Sparks slippers and sobbing uncontrollably into the sleeve of his beige Primark cardigan.

José Mourinho's Cool will be buried at the new Wembley Stadium. It is survived by José Mourinho's new range of polyester cardigans and slacks with elasticated waists and José Mourinho Dog Biscuits – 'For Your Special One'.

The People's Game

1863–2007

The People's Game has passed away as Liverpool FC, one of the last English football clubs actually capable of winning a soccer trophy beyond the award for 'Best Second Eleven Away Strip', was converted into a 'franchise' under overseas ownership.

Immensely popular throughout England almost from the moment of its creation, The People's Game was a simple entertainment, capable of uniting men up and down the country as they stood, cap on head and scarf round neck, in the terraces of a Sunday afternoon and shouted spirited encouragement to the members of their local team – most of whom were born and brought up within hailing distance of their home ground – and even more spirited imprecations against the rapscallions on the opposing side and the frailties of the person of questionable parentage in referee's uniform.

It was in the early 1990s that The People's Game began, like so many an England international, to drift slowly towards inevitable defeat in the penalty shoot-out of life. It was at that time that The Game first began its involvement with the notorious Americo-Australian lothario, Rupert Murdoch. Like Wedekind's *Lulu*, The People's Game soon found itself living a life of wild excess, throwing its money away on a parade of vacuous pretty boys and brutish thugs... many of whom would go on to play for England. Its appetites beyond satiation, even by Mr Murdoch's vast piles of cash, The People's Game was forced to go in search of more and more and richer and richer suitors, be they ageing American multimillionaires or billionaire Russian oligarchs. By the early noughties, The People's Game was even willing to sell off the most successful football club England had ever seen to anyone with a bit of cash to spare for a new stadium.

Yet even this was not the height of its infamy, for at the same time The People's Game was willing to do almost anything (except provide a team capable of winning the World Cup) to extract the last penny from the pockets of its fans. With its ticket prices soaring and sports rights being sold for astronomical fees, The People's Game eventually put itself beyond the reach of those who loved it, thrusting itself instead into the hands of corporate sponsors whose perfect view of a match was out of the corner of an eye while doing a deal in the VIP restaurant and far-flung 'fans' who were in less danger of visiting their team's stadium than Kettering FC are of winning the European cup.

The People's Game will be buried at the Church of St Lineker the Crisp-Seller. The Reverend Alan Hansen will read Psalm 4752 'The Defence Were Woeful and No One Tracked Back'. Well-wishers are asked to send as much cash as possible.

Tiger 'Tim' Henman

1974–2007

Tiger 'Tim' Henman, for many years Britain's greatest hope of ~~losing~~ winning Wimbledon, has gone to the Great Practice Court in the Sky having been knocked out of Wimbledon for the last time after years of being defeated by rain, injury, bad luck and – chiefly – not being quite good enough at tennis.

Tiger 'Tim' Henman was born in 1974, with a silver strawberry in his mouth – his father a keen tennis player and both his grandfather and great-grandfather competitors at Wimbledon, making their millions in the lucrative world of strawberries and cream concessions.

Slapped by the midwife, Tiger – so-called not because of his tenacious fighting spirit and ability to rip his opponents to shreds but because of his uncanny resemblance to the moth-eaten tiger-skin rug the family had inherited from Great Aunt Leticia – astounded his parents by returning his umbilical cord across the maternity room with a beautiful top-spin smash (although he later lost to the midwife 6–3, 6–3, 7–6, 7–6, 6–0).

From an early age Tiger was encouraged to follow his natural talent, but like most children he quickly rebelled and decided instead to become a tennis player, a pursuit in which his passionate displays earned him the equally passionate sobriquet 'Tim'.

Tiger rose rapidly through the junior tennis ranks thanks to his extraordinary skill and dedication and the fact that all the juniors who were any good at sport were playing football, rugby or training for athletics. Having mastered the basics of tennis – the serve, the volley, the sliced cross-court return (although until the end of his career he failed to convincingly punch the air like he meant it) – Tiger soon graduated to the seniors' circuit where he was greeted at Wimbledon as the second coming of the British tennis messiah and, everywhere else, as 'that useless Brit who doesn't even have the excuse that he's actually Canadian'.

Unlike many successful tennis players, Tiger refused to indulge in the competitive gamesmanship of his rivals and always remembered his manners, saying 'please' and 'thank you' but mostly 'sorry' to his fans and Sue Barker after every match. So, it was a surprise when, in his second Wimbledon tournament in 1995, he became the first player ever to be disqualified after smashing a ball into a ball girl's head (although the ball girl later won in straight sets).

Despite this Tiger captured the imagination of British fans desperate for a hero, completely ignorant of the rules of tennis and relishing only the chance to drape themselves in a Union Jack and bellow 'Do come on, Timothy' at a crucial point in the match – normally as their hero was returning a difficult first serve or trying to work out how to operate the Robinson's Barley Water dispenser. 'Henmania' reached fever pitch, climaxing with the christening of 'Henman Hill' – a scruffy mound on the verges of Wimbledon, nearly several feet high.

Tiger's frustrating losses on the Grand Slam circuit were easily compensated by his amazing Wimbledon performances – as year after year he was knocked out by the rain (or, in 2002, by wild card David Blunkett). But his gritty determination still won him the support of his fans as he clawed defeat from the jaws of victory, all the while punching the air (although he later lost to the air in straight sets in the first round of the French Open).

With the rise of tennis player Andy Murray, Tiger's status slipped and he became Britain's Number Two – a status his harsher critics had been euphemistically granting him for some time. At Wimbledon he valiantly fought his opponent, the weather and his own ineptitude, succumbing only after his Adidas wellingtons became stuck in the Centre Court mud. The spell was broken and his ~~mentally disturbed~~ loyal fans and the media realised Tiger had miaowed his last.

Tiger 'Tim' Henman will be buried at the Fred Perry Church of Nostalgia. The service will be too fast for him to return, but the congregation will struggle on as the final eulogy is delayed by rain for 24 hours before being knocked out in the last set.

He is predeceased by Greg Rusedski and survived by Andy Murray – the spotty 20-year-old with 'wrist injuries'.

Index

www.summersdale.com